SKILLS FOR BUSINESS ENGLISH

Student Book 2

Bill Mascull

DELTA PUBLISHING

Map of the book

UNIT	FUNCTIONS	SKILLS AND LANGUAGE FOCUS

1
Companies and products
Smart Kitchens: franchising in Australia
	Describing companies
	Describing products
	Complaining about poor performance
		A Listening
		  • vocabulary: company organisation and history; a company founder talking about her company; people talking about their work
		B Reading and writing
		  • describing products; reading an advertisement; responding by e-mail
		C Speaking
		  • complaining and responding; typical complaints
		Role play: an unpaid invoice

2
Travel and tourism
Golf in Crete: tourist development in Greece
	Telephoning
	Making arrangements
	Making reservations
		A Reading and writing
		  • tourism vocabulary; an article about a new tourist development; writing about a tourist destination
		B Listening
		  • telephone vocabulary; phone calls to fix a visit and make reservations
		C Speaking
		  • flying vocabulary; flight reservations
		Role play: confirming flight information

3
Economic trends
Hermosa: dilemmas of a growing Asian economy
	Economic development
	Dealing with figures
	Talking about graphs and trends
		A Listening
		  • vocabulary of the economy and industries; an interview about a developing country; describing graphs
		B Speaking
		  • graphs and charts vocabulary; comparisons and trends in the economy
		Pair work: exchanging economic information
		C Reading and writing
		  • vocabulary of economic growth; an article about an environmentally damaging development; writing a report

4
Employment and recruitment
Random Semiconductors: hi-tech investment in Ireland
	Manufacturing
	Advertising jobs
	CVs and interviews
	Signs at work
		A Reading and writing
		  • employment vocabulary; articles about a new plant; writing a job application
		B Reading and speaking
		  • production vocabulary; job advertisements
		Role plays: job interviews
		C Listening
		  • workplace vocabulary; warning signs; a plant tour

5
Competition
Flyaway: UK-based low-cost airline
	Giving opinions
	Entrepreneurs
	Exchanging information
		A Listening
		  • air passenger interviews; competition vocabulary; a low-cost airline
		B Speaking
		  • entrepreneurs and start-ups
		Role play: finding out about entrepreneurs
		C Reading and writing
		  • advice to people starting their own company; a letter to an entrepreneur from a source of finance; writing a reply

6
Better ways of working
Meblopol: Polish furniture for a world market
	The working environment
	Dealing with figures
	Suppliers, wholesalers and retailers
		A Listening
		  • vocabulary: ways of working; people talking about where they work; an interview about the working environment
		B Speaking
		  • vocabulary and expressions for ordering things
		Role plays: negotiating an order for office furniture
		C Reading and writing
		  • vocabulary: makers, sellers and buyers; an article about a furniture company; writing a letter to a buyer

UNIT	FUNCTIONS	SKILLS AND LANGUAGE FOCUS
7 Going for growth *Smart Kitchens: franchises, franchisees and their customers*	Lending and borrowing money Negotiating a loan Complaining about poor performance	A Reading and writing • vocabulary of growth; an article about franchising; an advertisement for franchisees; an e-mail request to become a franchisee B Speaking • vocabulary of lending and borrowing Role plays: becoming a franchisee; obtaining a bank loan C Listening • vocabulary of complaints; dealing with customer complaints; an interview with a bank executive about lending
8 Projects and schedules *Golf in Crete: project management and completion*	Social English Managing projects Describing location Describing accommodation	A Listening • expressions: arrival and greetings; discussion of a project; vocabulary: schedules; people talking about work schedules; project planning B Reading and writing • vocabulary: budgets; an article about completion of a new tourist development; writing a fax from a tour operator C Speaking • expressions: location; vocabulary: hotels Role plays: a tourist office; tour operators and tourists
9 In the news *Hermosa: development decisions and the environment*	Opposing and protesting Making your point Business news Accepting and rejecting proposals	A Listening • business news items; vocabulary: protest; environmental protest B Speaking • expressions: making your point; for and against; developing your point C Reading and writing • vocabulary: proposals; an internal memo in an environmental organisation; writing a letter to the organisation
10 Good times and bad *Random Semiconductors: hi-tech downturn*	Slumps and recessions Job cuts and redundancies Motivation and morale Career development	A Listening • boom and recession; levels of activity in different industries; vocabulary: redundancy; job losses at a company in difficulty B Reading and writing • language of human resources; a redundancy letter; writing a reply C Speaking • vocabulary: morale; questions and answers: career development Role plays: two employees discuss their plans; an employee talks to an outplacement agency
11 Takeovers and mergers *Flyaway merges with another airline*	Voicemail messages Plans and consequences Comparing and contrasting	A Listening • takeover and merger vocabulary; a takeover scenario B Reading and writing • comparing different companies; the results of mergers; writing an e-mail to a friend about a merger C Speaking • vocabulary of plans and their consequences; the planned benefits of mergers, and what actually happened Role play: comparing company cultures
12 Doing deals *Meblopol wins a big contract*	Social language Negotiation Reaching and confirming agreement	A Listening • saying hello and getting down to business; a meeting on a plane B Speaking and writing • negotiation expressions; commercial negotiation; writing an e-mail of confirmation Role play: negotiating C Reading and writing • vocabulary of commercial agreements • confirmation faxes

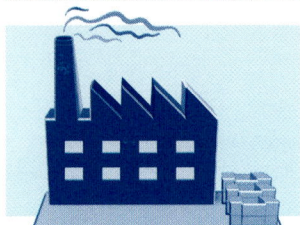

describing companies

describing products

complaining about poor performance

Companies and products

KEY VOCABULARY

Describing companies

When someone describes a company, they may talk about:

1. when it was started or **founded** and who its **founder** was
2. who runs the company: who its **chief executive** is
3. what **products** it makes or what **services** it provides
4. its **sales figures**
5. how many people work for it: how many **employees** it has
6. where its **headquarters** are: where it is **based**
7. where its **factories** or **plants** are located (if it's a manufacturing company)
8. how many **branches** or **retail outlets** (shops) it has (if it's a retail organisation)
9. whether it sells **business-to-business**, or whether it's a retail organisation selling to **consumers**
10. whether it uses a **franchising system**, where retail outlets are managed by individual owners called **franchisees** who have a share in the profits made by their **franchise**

A Listening

1. Talk briefly about the company you work for (or one you would like to work for), using the points above. Then make notes while other members of the group do the same.

2. 🎧 You are going to hear short extracts about four companies, mentioning some of the points above. Write the numbers of the points mentioned next to the extract letter. The first one has been done for you.

   A _3, 4, 6_   C _____

   B _____   D _____

4

3 🎧 Smart Kitchens is a company that has just won the Australian Business of the Year Award. Jane Smart, founder and Chief Executive, talks about the company in a business programme on the radio. Listen to the recording once, and say which of the points 1–10 on page 4 are mentioned.

4 Listen to the recording again and choose the correct alternative to answer the questions.

    1 Jane Smart started the company in _____.
      a) 1973   b) 1975   c) 1979

    2 She started the company in _____.
      a) Sydney   b) Melbourne   c) Perth

    3 Getting finance to start the company was _____.
      a) easy   b) difficult   c) impossible

    4 Her colleagues Rebecca and Jim _____.
      a) are still with the company
      b) have left the company
      c) have started another company

    5 Smart Kitchens and its franchisees now have _____.
      a) 7 showrooms and 300 employees
      b) 20 showrooms and 500 employees
      c) 30 showrooms and 600 employees

    6 About how much of the company's business is with people who have just moved?
      a) 25%   b) 50%   c) 75%

    7 In the early 1990s, Smart Kitchens had to _____.
      a) employ more staff
      b) keep the same number of staff
      c) get rid of staff

    8 How many of its branches does Smart Kitchens own and run directly?
      a) five   b) seven   c) ten

    9 What is the most important way in which the company can help its franchisees?
      a) through supplying materials
      b) through its computer system
      c) through advice on employing and training employees

   10 In talking about how to succeed in setting up a business, what subject does Jane Smart *not* talk about?
      a) market research
      b) employing the right people
      c) having a good relationship with a bank

5 🎧 Listen to six people talking about their work in the Smart Kitchens headquarters in Melbourne. Mark the statements T (for True) or F (for False).

	T	F
1 Rebecca deals mainly with new franchises.	T	F
2 Jim is an engineer by training.	T	F
3 Sandra deals mainly with the showrooms that Smart Kitchens manage directly.	T	F
4 Don works on designing kitchens.	T	F
5 Anna has a lot of contact with franchisees.	T	F
6 Douglas has been with the company a long time.	T	F

Reading and writing

Describing products

Among the words in the box describing products, find:

a) two words relating to appearance
b) two words meaning that something is new and unlike existing products
c) two words meaning that a product does something without wasting time and energy
d) one word meaning that something does not break easily
e) one word meaning that something does not break down easily
f) one word meaning that something is small and easy to carry
g) one word meaning that something is strong and works with a lot of force

beautiful	compact	economical	efficient	good-looking
innovative	powerful	reliable	revolutionary	robust

1 Look at the advertisement from *Modern Kitchens* magazine and choose the correct word from 1–11 on page 7 to complete each gap. Only one of the words is possible in each case.

DO YOU SPEND A LOT OF TIME IN THE KITCHEN?

Metro

Rio

It's where most Australian families eat these days, and you want it to be just the way you like it, with everything you need to make your kitchen somewhere inviting and (1) _____.
And when you're cooking, you want things to be as (2) _____ as possible, and easy to clean and (3) _____ as well, of course. With all those new exotic dishes you see on those cooking programmes on TV, cooking can be quite (4) _____ these days, and you want all the help you can get, and the best advice that there is!

Smart Kitchens has been (5) _____ and (6) _____ kitchens for 30 years.

Whether you live in a house or a flat, whatever the (7) _____ of your kitchen, we have the answer.

Our kitchens are made from the finest (8) _____. We look all over the world for the (9) _____, state-of-the-art equipment.

Contact us and one of our highly (10) _____ team of (11) _____ will come round to discuss the possibilities. Just contact one of our showrooms below. There's at least one in every major Australian city.

1 a) counterfeit   b) comfortable   c) considerate   d) complimentary
2 a) available   b) commodious   c) contemplative   d) convenient
3 a) mainstay   b) maintain   c) mainline   d) mainspring
4 a) competed   b) completed   c) complicated   d) compliant
5 a) designating   b) designing   c) desiring   d) dissecting
6 a) installing   b) instigating   c) instilling   d) insisting
7 a) sigh   b) sight   c) sign   d) size
8 a) matters   b) materials   c) masters   d) materiel
9 a) latest   b) last   c) lasting   d) lasted
10 a) professor   b) professional   c) professing   d) professed
11 a) drawers   b) designators   c) designating   d) designers

2 Look at this advertisement for Smart Kitchens. In each numbered line (1–6) there is one extra word that does not fit. Cross out the extra word. The first line has been done as an example.

1 ~~The~~ one of our most popular models is the Rustic.
2 The Rustic is like the kitchen your grandmother knew. This kitchen it has
3 beautiful working surfaces, but they are easy to clean. There are of flower designs
4 on the cupboards. Modern equipment is hidden behind old-style doors. Lighting is a
5 soft and subtle. On the floor, there are old-fashioned tiles, but made with off modern
6 materials and easy to on maintain.

Just phone us on (03) 9325 7300, fax us on (03) 9325 7350, or e-mail John Burke at info@smartkitchens.com for a no-obligation visit. Nationwide service.

3 Look at this e-mail to Smart Kitchens asking for a visit by one of their designers.

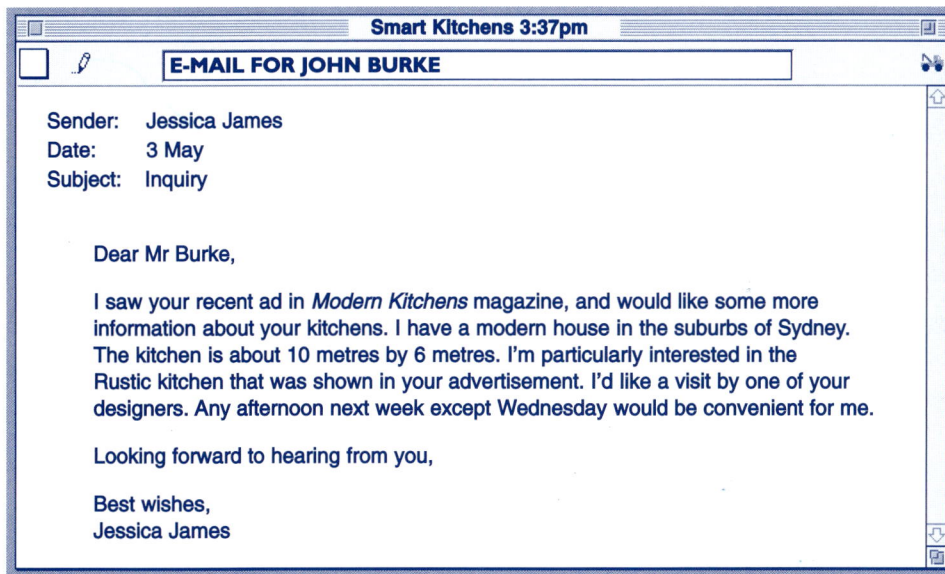

Smart Kitchens 3:37pm

E-MAIL FOR JOHN BURKE

Sender: Jessica James
Date: 3 May
Subject: Inquiry

Dear Mr Burke,

I saw your recent ad in *Modern Kitchens* magazine, and would like some more information about your kitchens. I have a modern house in the suburbs of Sydney. The kitchen is about 10 metres by 6 metres. I'm particularly interested in the Rustic kitchen that was shown in your advertisement. I'd like a visit by one of your designers. Any afternoon next week except Wednesday would be convenient for me.

Looking forward to hearing from you,

Best wishes,
Jessica James

Now write a similar e-mail with your own details, including:

* the type of property you have (house or flat)
* approximate dimensions of your kitchen (in metres)
* the name of the kitchen you are interested in (among the three styles featured in the ads)
* which days and times next week would be suitable for a designer to visit
* which days and times next week would not be possible for a visit

Close appropriately.

KEY EXPRESSIONS AND QUESTIONS
Complaining about poor performance

I'm calling/phoning/writing to complain about ...
There's some sort of delay/hold-up/problem.
There seems to be a problem with ...
Things are in a mess.
Something has gone wrong somewhere.
There seems to be a problem in the system.
I'd like to make a formal complaint.

What's going on?
Can you tell me what's happening?
Who's in charge of this?
Could you look into this?

Responding to complaints

I'll look into this and get back to you.
My colleague Mr/Ms X deals with this. I'll get him/her to call you back.
I'm afraid there's been a problem with ...
I'm sorry about this. We've changed our procedures so it won't happen again.
We apologise for the mistake. It won't happen again.
Our apologies for the mix-up. We've sorted things out now.
We've looked into your complaint and it seems to be justified. Can we offer you
some sort of compensation?

1 Look at these typical complaints. For each one, add
two more things that can go wrong.

Delivery of goods

1 the wrong goods are delivered

2 the goods are delivered to the wrong place

3 _____

4 _____

Product performance: computers

1 the computer doesn't work at all

2 the computer works, but very slowly

3 _____

4 _____

Service performance: car mechanics

1 the mechanic doesn't fix the fault

2 they fix the fault but another fault appears

3 _____

4 _____

Service performance: banks

1 you order a cheque book, but it never arrives

2 the bank takes money from your account as "service charges" without explaining what they are

3 _____

4 _____

Product and service performance: clothes

1 you buy a pair of trousers; you try them on at home and they're too tight, but the shop refuses to exchange them

2 you notice a small defect (manufacturing mistake) in a jacket, which otherwise you really like, and you ask if you can have a discount, but the shop assistant doesn't offer one

3 _____

4 _____

2 Describe to a partner a situation where you have made a complaint, perhaps like one of the ones in Exercise 1. Make notes below about the people involved and the steps you took.

What went wrong exactly? _____

Who did you complain to? _____

How did they react? _____

Was the complaint dealt with satisfactorily by this person? _____

What was the final outcome? _____

Now role play the situation in pairs. B makes the complaint and A responds.

3 This role play is for two speakers.

A is the head of a small firm (three employees) that does a lot of its business with a big multinational. In fact, sales to the multinational are half of the firm's total sales.

The multinational usually pays suppliers 60 days after receiving the invoice.

A has been waiting for the payment of an invoice for a very large amount of money ($50,000) for nearly three months.

B works in the accounts payable department of the multinational.

A makes a series of phone calls to B to enquire about the payment.

A looks at this page. B turns to page 76. Read and prepare your part, then talk to your partner.

SPEAKER A

June 1:   Phone to ask about the invoice. Say that payment is two weeks overdue.

June 8:   Still no call from B. Phone them to ask what's happening.

June 20: You still haven't received the cheque. Cashflow is getting to be a real problem. You will not be able to pay the June salaries of your three employees unless you receive payment. Complain again, more strongly.

July 6:   Still no payment. You lose your temper. You now risk going out of business. Ask to speak to the head of the accounts payable department.

Travel and tourism

telephoning

making arrangements

making reservations

KEY VOCABULARY

Tourism

Choose the correct alternative to complete the sentences.

1   The period of the year when most visitors normally go to a particular place
    is the tourist _____.
    a) season   b) phase   c) duration

2   An organisation that offers holidays for people is a tour _____.
    a) supplier   b) provider   c) operator

3   A flight specially for people going on holiday in a particular place,
    where all the seats have been paid for in advance by travel companies, is
    a/an _____.
    a) group flight   b) charter flight   c) unscheduled flight

4   Another name for a hotel owner is a _____.
    a) hotelier   b) hoteller   c) hotellist

5   Buildings, equipment, services, etc designed for use by tourists are
    tourist _____.
    a) premises   b) facilities   c) penitentiaries

6   The money that foreign tourists spend in a country is a source of
    foreign _____.
    a) excess   b) expenditure   c) exchange

A   Reading and writing

1   Read the article on page 11.
    Choose the best title for each numbered paragraph from a–g below. Do not use
    any letter more than once.

    Paragraph 1 _____   Paragraph 3 _____

    Paragraph 2 _____   Paragraph 4 _____

    a) A new golf course near Khania
    b) Crete's tourist season
    c) Developing a wider choice of activities in Crete
    d) Golf construction techniques
    e) Greece's efforts to compete with rival tourist destinations
    f) Greek golfing traditions
    g) The development of Turkish tourism

About 11 million visitors went to Greece last year, 10 per cent more than the previous year. Most tourists take charter flights to the islands of Crete, Corfu and Rhodes, or to Halkidiki on the northern Greek mainland. Tourism is Greece's biggest industry, earning the country about $8 billion annually in foreign exchange.

1   Crete is one of the most southerly islands and a popular holiday destination in spring and summer, but the tourist season is short, despite the fact that the winters are as warm as in countries like Tunisia and Morocco, which have large numbers of visitors in winter.

2   The Greek tourist industry is facing increasing competition from these countries and from neighbouring Turkey. The Greek National Tourist Organisation is trying to respond to this by developing activities that are not normally associated with Greece. Golf is one of them, and the GNTO is developing golf courses on state-owned land near the big tourist centres.

3   The Director of the Crete Hoteliers' Association, Mr Stavros Milatos, says, "At the moment the tourist season ends in November and we have to offer tourists a wider choice of activities. We want to invest in facilities that can be used all year round."

4   Tour operators and hotel owners in the port town of Khania are investing heavily. A group of 40 hoteliers have put up a considerable investment to build an 18-hole golf course near the town, one of the first golf courses on Crete. The course, to be designed and laid out by an American company, will be used mostly in the winter months as summer temperatures can reach 35°C and it's too hot to play golf during most of the day.

2 Using the information in the text, complete each sentence with a phrase (a–g) from the list below.

1 The Greek National Tourist Organisation wants to _____.

2 Greek hotel owners don't want to _____.

3 The Greek tourist industry _____.

4 Eleven million tourists _____.

a) is facing increased competition from other countries
b) develop Athens as a tourist destination
c) make the tourist season longer by encouraging people to visit in winter
d) came on charter flights last year
e) spend their time playing golf
f) invest in facilities that are not used all year round
g) went to Greece last year

3 Write about a tourist destination that you know. Using vocabulary from above, mention:

- where it is
- how to get there
- the climate
- when the main tourist season is
- the hotels
- the other facilities: restaurants, entertainment, sport, etc
- what developments there have been over the last ten or twenty years

KEY VOCABULARY

Telephoning

Look at these stages of making a **phone call**.

1 You **pick up the phone** and **dial the number**.
2 The number **rings** and someone **answers the phone**.
3 The number's **busy**, or (in British English) **engaged**.
4 If it's a **direct line**, the person who answers is normally the person you want to speak to. If they're not there, and they have **voicemail**, you can **leave a message** for them.
5 You dial someone's direct line, but a colleague of theirs answers. They say that the person you want to speak to is **on another line** and ask if you want to leave a message.
6 If it's not a direct line, you ask the **switchboard** to **put you through to** the extension you want.
7 Sometimes there's a **recorded message** telling you to dial the extension yourself if you know it.
8 You talk to the person you want, but suddenly you're **cut off**: you can't hear them and they can't hear you. You **redial** the number and try to **reach** them again.
9 You end the conversation and **hang up**.

1 🎧 Listen to six extracts from telephone calls. Match each extract (A–F) with one of the situations (1–9) above.

A _____   C _____   E _____

B _____   D _____   F _____

2 🎧 Golf Course Design and Construction Inc (GCDC) is a US company based in Raleigh, North Carolina. Its CEO (Chief Executive Officer) is Alvin Palmer and he has already been in contact by phone and e-mail with Stavros Milatos of the Crete Hoteliers' Association about the construction of a golf course near Khania in Crete.

Listen to the recording and mark the statements T (for true), F (for false), or DK (we don't know).

1 When Palmer calls Milatos, he gets put through immediately.	T	F	DK
2 The weather in Crete is good.	T	F	DK
3 The weather in Raleigh is good.	T	F	DK
4 Palmer has sent Milatos a very detailed proposal.	T	F	DK
5 Milatos has been in touch with four other companies about the project.	T	F	DK
6 Palmer and Milatos discuss the costs of the project.	T	F	DK
7 Palmer suggests that Milatos visits Raleigh.	T	F	DK
8 Palmer has been to Greece before on holiday.	T	F	DK
9 Palmer may be coming with someone else when he visits Crete.	T	F	DK
10 Milatos suggests that Palmer should fly to Khania.	T	F	DK

3 Listen to the recording again and underline the words you actually hear on the recording. The first one has been done for you.

1 May I speak to Mr Milatos, please? / <u>Can I speak to Mr Milatos, please?</u>

2 I'll put you through. / I'm putting you through.

3 Hi, Stavros, it's Al Palmer. How are you? / Hi, Stavros, this is Al Palmer. How are you?

4 How's the weather over there? / How's the weather with you?

5 Of course, there are some things we must talk about in more detail. / Of course, there are some points we must talk about in more detail.

6 That's inevitable. But you like the general idea? / That's inevitable. But you like the overall idea?

7 How about coming over here to discuss things in the next couple of weeks? / What about coming over here to discuss things in the next couple of weeks?

8 It'll be great to see you over here. / It'll be good to see you over here.

9 We'll arrange for someone to meet you. / We'll arrange for someone to pick you up.

10 OK, my personal assistant will contact you soon with our arrangements. / OK, my personal assistant will be in touch soon with our arrangements.

4 🎧 Listen to Alvin Palmer's personal assistant making the hotel reservation for his trip, and complete the information below.

Name of hotel: _____

Names of guests: _____

Date of arrival: _____

Date of departure: _____

Room rate: _____

Breakfast included? _____

Special requests: _____

Hotel's e-mail address: _____

C Speaking

Flying and flight reservations

Combine the words on the left with the words on the right to form compounds that match definitions a–f below.

1	arrivals	number
2	check-in	flight
3	connecting	desk
4	departure	hall
5	flight	passengers
6	transfer	lounge

a) people at an airport who have just arrived there on a flight and are flying on to somewhere else.

b) a very large room at an airport for passengers who have just arrived, people meeting them, etc

c) the number identifying the aeroplane and route

d) the place where you tell the airline that you have arrived for your flight

e) the room where passengers wait just before they get on the plane

f) the second or third flight that you take as part of one journey

1 Talk about these three ways of getting from London to Istanbul, being especially careful with numbers, times and prices.

London Heathrow to Istanbul direct (all times are local)

	British Airways flight BA310	Turkish Airlines flight TL509
London dep	09.00	15.15
Istanbul arr	14.35	20.05

London Heathrow to Istanbul via Paris (all times are local)

	Air France
London dep	11.25 AF430
Paris arr	13.10
Paris dep	14.30 AF573
Istanbul arr	18.30

Fares (in euros)

	British Airways	Turkish Airlines	Air France
Business class return	1050	1050	1050
Economy return	695	665	620
APEX* return	350	320	310

*Advance Purchase Excursion (no changes possible once booked)

2 This role play is for two speakers.

A is Alvin Palmer's personal assistant (PA). She is making arrangements for Palmer's trip from Raleigh to Khania, Crete.

B is a travel agent.

A looks at this page. B turns to page 76.

SPEAKER A

You have received a fax from the travel agent with flight times from Raleigh to Crete, but unfortunately some of the details are impossible to read.

Phone the travel agent (B) to complete the information and to get them to confirm:
* the cost of each option
* the arrival and departure time of each flight
* where you have to change planes
* how long you have to wait in each place
* what time you finally get to Khania

fax ···

Option 1

COST ~~$4,847.0~~
Business class round trip
▶ MetroJet flight 2784 on a Boeing 737-200
 From: Raleigh/Durham, Monday Dec 3, dep ~~~~
 To: ~~~~, arr 17.59

Olympic flight 416 on a Boeing 747;
1 stop (in Frankfurt: ~~~~)
 From: Boston, Monday Dec 3, dep ~~~~
 To: ~~Athens~~, Greece, Tuesday Dec 4, arr 12.55

Cronus Airlines flight 404 on a Boeing 737-400
 From: Athens, Greece, Tuesday Dec 4, dep ~~~~
 To: ~~~~, Crete, arr 15.45

Option 2

COST $4,884.20
Business class round trip
▶ American Airlines flight 174 on a Boeing 767
 From: Raleigh/Durham, Monday Dec 3, dep ~~~~
 To: ~~~~, Tuesday Dec 4, arr ~~~~

Virgin Atlantic flight 1002 on an Airbus Industrie
~~~~
 From: ~~~~, Tuesday Dec 4, dep ~~~~
 To: Athens, Greece, arr ~~~~

Cronus Airlines flight 406 on a Boeing 737-400
 From: Athens, Greece, Tuesday Dec 4, dep ~~~~
 To: Khania, Crete, arr ~~~~

Economic trends

economic development

dealing with figures

talking about graphs
and trends

KEY VOCABULARY

The economy

Match the expressions on the left with the definitions on the right.

1 manufacturing
2 services
3 gross domestic
  product (GDP)
4 GDP per head
5 currency
6 exchange rate
7 inflation
8 unemployment

A the total value of goods and services produced
  divided by the total number of people in the country
B rising prices
C the situation of not having a job when you want
  one
D the value of a currency in relation to other
  currencies
E the part of an economy related to making things
F the total value of all the goods and services
  produced in the country in a year
G the part of an economy not related to making things,
  but to providing finance, leisure activities, etc
H the money used in a particular country

Industries

Match the names of the manufacturing and service industries with what they
make or do.

1 banking
2 construction
3 electronics
4 media
5 steel
6 textiles
7 tourism

A making cloth and clothes
B providing holidays
C making a stronger, more valuable metal out of iron
D building roads, factories, houses, etc
E making parts used in computers, televisions, mobile
  phones, etc
F providing finance
G making and distributing films, television
  programmes, etc

A Listening

1 🎧 Listen to an interview with Rebecca Chu (a specialist on the country of Hermosa)
  on a business programme on the radio. Complete the information below.

Hermosa

Official name: Democratic Republic of Hermosa
Location: western Pacific
Area: 200,000 square kilometres
Population: 40 million
Capital and main port: Merida
Outline history: discovered and colonised by the
  (1) _Spanish_ in the (2) _70_th century. Independence
  in 1898.
Ethnic groups: native Hermosans (3) _40_%, Hispanics
(4) _30_%, Chinese (5) _20_%, Indians (6) _6_%, others 4%

Languages: (7) _Spanish_, (8) _Chinese_, (9) _Hindi_
  and, increasingly, English
Growth this year: (10) _5.6_ %
Current unemployment: (11) _4_ %
Current inflation: (12) _3_ %
Currency: Hermosan peso
Current exchange rate: (13) _32_ pesos to the
  US dollar
Important industries today: (14) _Tourism_
  (15) _Electronics_

16

2 Practise the key language for describing graphs by completing the different grammatical forms.

Base form of verb	past simple	past participle	noun
go up	went up	gone up	—
rise	rose	rissen	rise
increase	increased	increased	increase
grow	grew	grown	growth
go down	went down	gone down	—
fall	fell	fallen	fall
decrease.	decreased	decreased	decrease
drop	dropped	dropped	drop
reach	reached	reached.	—

3 🎧 Rebecca Chu is giving a lecture to her students about trends in the Hermosan economy. Use the information you hear to complete the graphs below.

A GDP per head

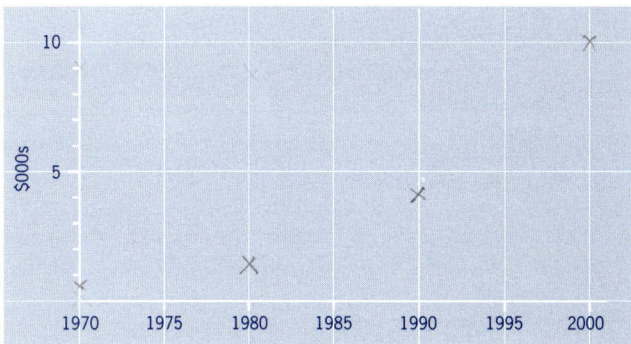

B Life expectancy

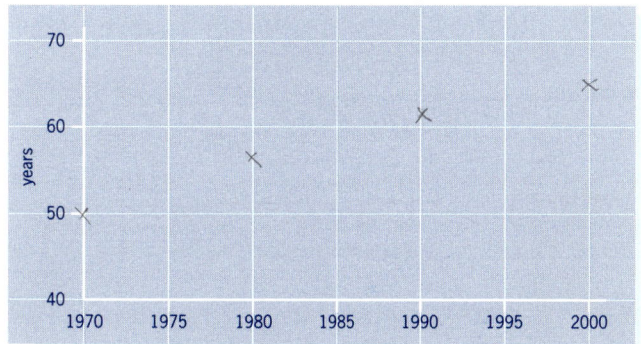

C Adult literacy

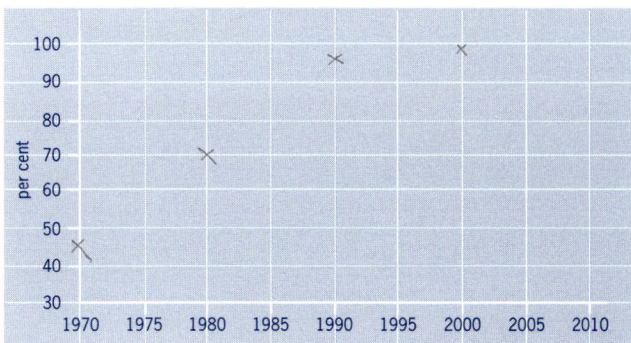

D Number of cars per 100 people

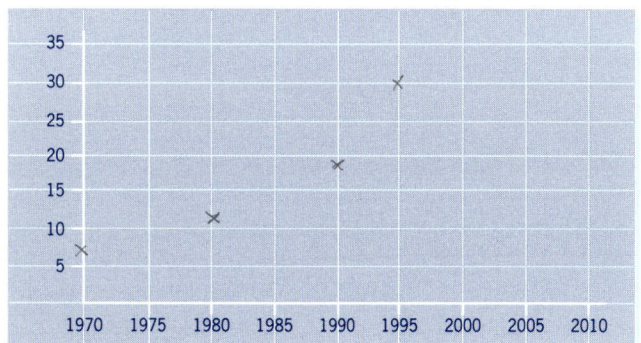

E Number of people per television set

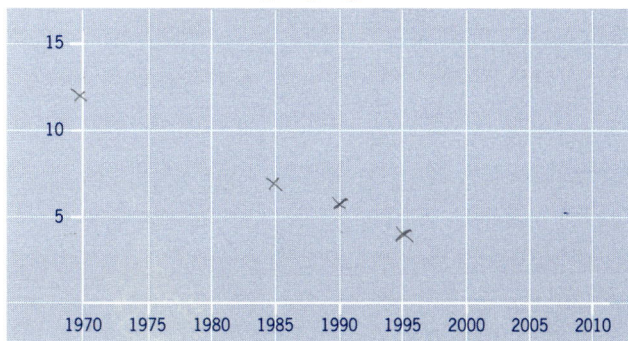

B   Speaking

Graphs and charts

Label the drawings with the words in the box.

| pie chart | bar chart | line graph | vertical axis | horizontal axis |

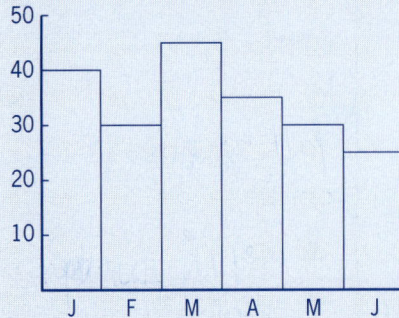

1 _____

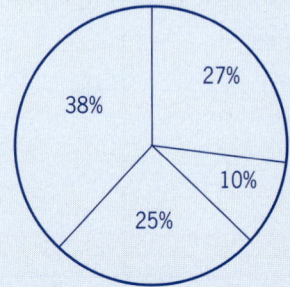

2 _____

3 _____

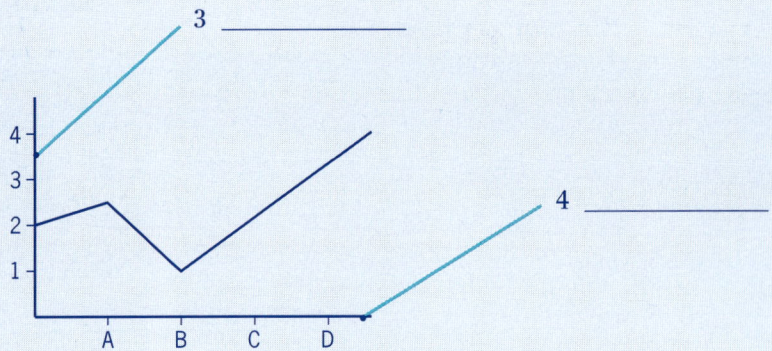

4 _____

5 _____

Comparisons and trends

Choose the correct alternative to complete the sentences.

1 _____ people own cars.

   a) more and more   b) the more and the more   c) most and most

2 _____ people are illiterate.

   a) few and few   b) fewer and fewer   c) fewest and fewest

3 More people work in tourism _____ in steel.

   a) this   b) that   c) than

4 _____ people are employed in agriculture than in industry.

   a) few   b) fewer   c) fewest

5 Unemployment reached a _____ of 8% of the workforce, and then it fell.

   a) height   b) top   c) peak

6 Growth reached a _____ point of only 1% that year, but then it increased.

   a) down   b) low   c) foot

7 Inflation reached 5% but then it levelled _____ and stayed at the same percentage for some time.

   a) in   b) off   c) on

1 These pair work activities are for two speakers.

In activities 1 and 3, A describes the graph or pie chart, and B uses this information to complete the graph or pie chart on page 77.

In activities 2 and 4, B describes the graph or pie chart on page 77 and A uses the information to complete the graph or pie chart on this page.

A look at this page. B turns to page 77.

1 Gross Domestic Product per head in Hermosa and its neighbours

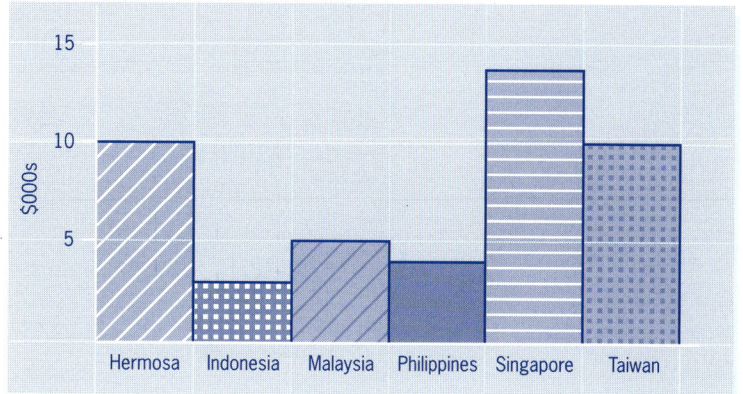

2 Population of Hermosa's major cities: Merida, Vallarta and Newport
(graph with three lines)

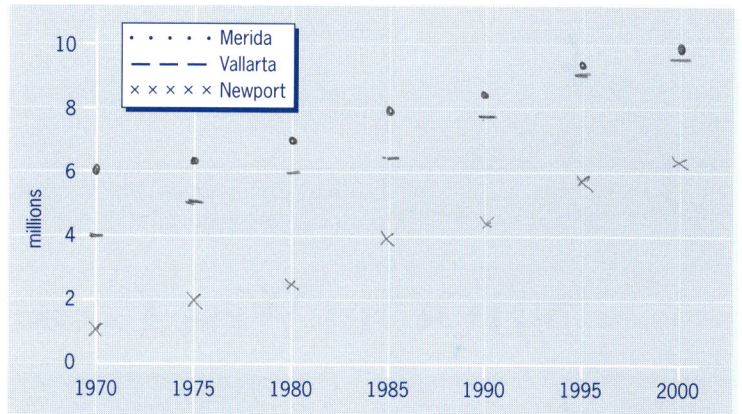

3 Hermosa: cinema visits per person per year

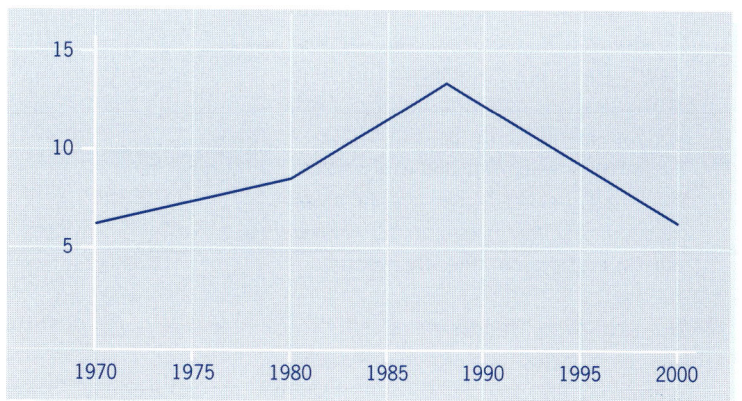

4 Hermosa's workforce
(pie chart)

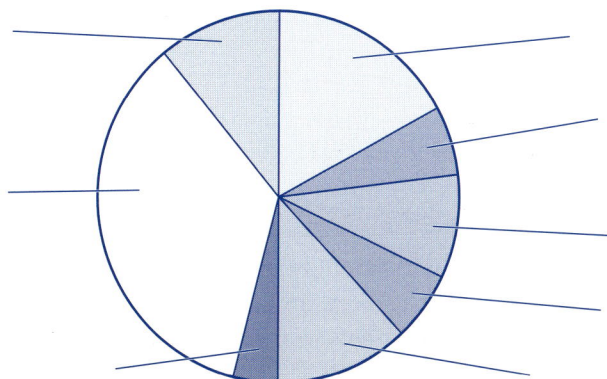

Economic development

Complete the commentary using the words in the box.

> development   environment   living standards   prosperous
> poverty   prosperity   quality of life   stress

Economic growth is when industrial activity develops and people have more money and better (1) _living standards_ there is a rise in people's (2) _prosperity_. There may be improvements in health and people may live longer, but some say that there is a price to pay in terms of damage to the (3) _environment_, with polluted air and water, and also in terms of (4) _quality of life_: people start to lead busy city lives and get new diseases caused by (5) _stress_, and by eating new foods they did not eat when they lived in the country.

Others say that it's easy to idealise the life of poor farming families, a life that is really one of ignorance and (6) _poverty_. They say that economic (7) _development_ is the only way out of this, and that as people get more (8) _prosperous_, they will demand a cleaner environment, forcing companies to repair the damage caused in increasing the country's wealth.

1 Read this article from the English-language daily *The Hermosa Times*, and mark the statements T (for true), F (for false) or DK (we don't know).

NHOC in West Coast Refinery Shock

1 The National Hermosa Oil Corporation (NHOC) officially announced yesterday that it intends to construct a $1 billion oil refinery on the west coast of the island. The project is expected to take five years to complete, with 2,000 workers involved in its construction. The refinery when finished will employ 500 staff, easing the employment situation on the west coast, where tourism is at present the only industry.

2 Mr Ken Woo, president of NHOC, said at a press conference officially announcing the project, "The construction of the refinery is a vital step forward in the development of the economy of the island. It will bring much-needed jobs to the west coast and act as a motor for economic activity there."

3 The refinery is to be built 120 km north of Newport, near the small resort of Puerto Escondido, in the West Coast National

The site of the proposed oil refinery

Park. Ms Lucia Buenavista, a spokeswoman for the Ministry of the Environment, said that it "did not foresee difficulty" in giving planning permission for the project. She said that the ministry had been assured by NHOC that environmental controls would be extremely strict and that danger of oil pollution from the refinery was "minimal".

4 Local residents are less optimistic. The head of the environmental group Green Action, Mr Charles Chang, says that the prospect of large oil tankers unloading their cargo at the port is "alarming". "We don't believe what NHOC and the Ministry of the Environment are telling us. We've already seen the damage that oil pollution can do in other parts of the world. And the idea of building the refinery in a national park is ridiculous. What is the point of national parks if they can build oil refineries in them?"

1 It is estimated that the refinery will take five years to complete.   T   F   DK
2 The refinery will employ 2,000 people when it is completed.   T   F   DK
3 The refinery will employ 500 people in its construction.   T   F   DK
4 The refinery has been designed for an operating life of 75 years.   T   F   DK

   5 The president of NHOC announced the refinery during a
      television interview.   T   F   DK
   6 There is a shortage of jobs on the west coast.   T   F   DK
   7 He believes the refinery will have positive effects on the west
      coast economy.   T   F   DK
   8 He himself believes there is no danger of pollution from the
      refinery.   T   F   DK
   9 The Ministry of the Environment spokeswoman thinks the
      refinery will be given planning permission.   T   F   DK
  10 She believes that there is absolutely no danger of pollution
      from the refinery.   T   F   DK
  11 Charles Chang does not believe what NHOC and the Ministry
      of the Environment say.   T   F   DK
  12 Other industrial activities already exist in the West Coast
      National Park, apart from tourism.   T   F   DK

2 Now choose the best one-sentence summary for each paragraph of the article
   from this list. Write the number of the paragraph next to each summary.
   If a summary is not used, put a cross (✗).

   a) The head of Green Action gives his view of the development. _____

   b) The cost and numbers of workers involved in construction of the new refinery
      are given. _____

   c) The economic benefits of similar developments in other parts of the world are
      discussed. _____

   d) *The Hermosa Times* gives its view of whether the refinery should go ahead. _____

   e) The Ministry of the the Environment's spokeswoman says that the refinery will
      probably go ahead. _____

   f) The president of NHOC talks about the economic benefits of the refinery. _____

3 This is a report by the president of the West Coast Preservation Society on the
   planned refinery. In each numbered line (1–6), there is one extra word that does
   not fit. Cross out the extra word. The first line has been done as an example.

   1   News of the construction of a refinery ~~in~~ on the west coast is extremely

   2   worrying. We cannot allow the whole island to be covered in the concrete and

   3   industrial plants. Our economic development in the last 30 years is has been

   4   magnificent but we have to do make sure that the beauty of our island is kept for

   5   future for generations to enjoy. We should oppose this development as

   6   strongly as we can to. The whole future of our island is in danger if we allow

       this development to go ahead.

4 Write a continuation of the report in Exercise 3 of about 75 words, mentioning the
   following points:

   • Write about specific dangers to particular activities, eg tourism and the fishing
     industry.
   • Say what people should do in order to protest against the project: write to the
     Ministry of the Environment, organise petitions (where large numbers of people sign
     a statement against the project), organise street demonstrations, etc.
   • Finish by saying that more people see the need for protecting the environment and
     that with enough organised protest, the project will be defeated.

Employment and recruitment

manufacturing

advertising jobs

CVs and interviews

signs at work

Employment

Combine the words on the left with the words on the right to form compounds that match definitions a–e below.

1	inward	drive
2	job	investment
3	recruitment	creation
4	skilled	industry
5	hi-tech	workforce

a) efforts by a company to find people to work for it

b) a technically advanced business activity

c) employees and possible employees in a place with a good level of knowledge and abilities

d) money coming into a country, area, etc to be invested

e) when new jobs are made available in an organisation, region, etc

A   Reading and writing

1   Read this article and choose the correct alternative to fill each gap.

FEBRUARY 3, 2000   **IRISH DAILY**   PAGE 3

RANDOM DEVELOPMENT

Random Semiconductors, the Asian chip manufacturer, is understood to have (1) _____ an agreement with the Irish government for a new 1.6 billion euro (about $1.7 billion) microchip (2) _____ that would employ 1,000 people on a site ten miles outside Dublin. The plant is expected to open in early 2002.

Five sites in Europe and Asia were (3) _____ for the investment, and the final choice was between Ireland and a site in Malaysia. Mr Young Jin Park, head of global manufacturing for Random, said yesterday, "We have

chosen Ireland as an ideal (4) _____ with good links by air to the rest of Europe and for its highly skilled workforce. There are already a large number of hi-tech firms in the Dublin area and we are very pleased to add our presence here. And of course, there's the (5) _____ of life here: Ireland has the best golf courses in the world: a big attraction for our (6) _____ Asian managers."

The plant will manufacture the next generation of semi-conductors: the increasingly (7) _____ chips for consumer products such as watches,

TV sets, mobile phones and personal computers.

Random Semiconductors had world-wide sales of $2.75 billion last year, a 7.2% increase on the (8) _____ year. The company is the seventh (9) _____ semi-conductor manufacturer in the world.

The amount of inward investment into Ireland has been growing very fast recently, with an (10) _____ of 12% last year compared to the previous year.

1 a) done	b) fabricated	c) reached	d) produced
2 a) plant	b) farm	c) office	d) refinery
3 a) chosen	b) shortlisted	c) recruited	d) eliminated
4 a) placement	b) premises	c) plot	d) location
5 a) feeling	b) quality	c) goodness	d) atmosphere
6 a) expatriate	b) excessive	c) excited	d) exported
7 a) potent	b) potential	c) powered	d) powerful
8 a) earlier	b) precedent	c) previous	d) last
9 a) big	b) bigger	c) biggest	d) greater
10 a) increase	b) increases	c) increased	d) increasing

2 Look at this article about the new Random plant in Ireland. In each numbered line (1–10) there is one wrong word. Underline the word and write the correct word in the space. The first one has been done as an example.

NOVEMBER 20, 2000   **IRISH DAILY**   PAGE 4

RANDOM PLANT AHEAD OF SCHEDULE

Work is progressing well at the Random semiconductor plant and it is expected to

1 opened next month, two months ahead of schedule, employing about 1,000 people.   *open*

2 Helen O'Donnelly, employment consultant with longing experience of hi-tech   _____

3 recruitment, says she expects about half of these jobs will be high skilled, with   _____

4 priority being given to those with experiments of working in a hi-tech   _____

5 environment. "Of course, chip production is highly automation, and Random will   _____

6 need people used to working with very sophisticated equipments," Ms O'Donnelly   _____

7 says. Jobs centres throughout the Dublin area have posters telling people about the   _____

8 opportunities at Random's semiconductor plant. "There has been a hugely   _____

9 response," said Kate Murphy, district manager of the Irish govern's   _____

10 Employment Service for the Dublin area. "The projection will have an enormous   _____

impact on the job market in and around Dublin."

3 Write a letter to the head of recruitment at Random, asking about the possibility of working there. Say:

• that you saw a newspaper article about Random's new plant
• what type of job you are interested in
• when you are available to start
• what sort of background you have (use your own or invent one)
• that you are enclosing your CV

Close appropriately.

B   Reading and speaking

KEY VOCABULARY

Production

Match the expressions on the left with the definitions on the right.

1	continuous supply	A	the basic things needed to make something
2	equipment maintenance	B	making things using the latest techniques
3	safety standards	C	when the materials needed to make something are available all the time
4	raw materials	D	making sure that machines always work properly
5	key suppliers	E	rules designed to avoid accidents
6	materials inventory	F	the stock of things waiting to be used in production
7	advanced manufacturing	G	the most important companies that provide materials

1 Look at these advertisements for jobs at Random Semiconductors. Underline the expressions from the *Key vocabulary* above.

A

PRODUCTION SUPERVISOR

You will supervise and assist in the recruiting of operators. You will help maintain safety standards and communicate equipment and production problems to staff in engineering, management and equipment maintenance as necessary. You must have a business or technical degree with some direct supervision experience in the semiconductor industry. Excellent people management and leadership skills required.

C

EQUIPMENT MAINTENANCE TECHNICIAN

You will repair and maintain semi-conductor manufacturing equipment and support production engineers in limiting production losses. You must be capable of clearly recording all work performed. Five years' experience of working in a similar position required, not necessarily in the semiconductor industry. Technical qualification desirable but not essential.

B

BUYER / PLANNER

You will ensure the continuous supply of raw materials while minimising the raw materials inventory, dealing with key suppliers. You will negotiate cost reductions with suppliers and report progress monthly to senior management. You must be able to communicate and work closely with a variety of people, including scientists, engineers and senior managers. Minimum of 3 years' experience is required in either planning or purchasing, not necessarily in the semiconductor industry. Business degree desirable.

D

TRAINING MANAGER

to head a team of 10 technical trainers. In your mid to late 30s, you probably have a degree in electronic engineering or advanced manufacturing and clear leadership qualities and communication skills. You will take charge of basic technical training at Random. Experience of training in a semiconductor environment preferable.

2 Which job or jobs does each of these sentences refer to?

1 You have to be a good leader. _____

2 You don't need a degree, but having one would help. _____

3 You must have experience of the semiconductor industry. _____

4 Communication skills are not specifically mentioned. _____

5 You need to be able to get on with a wide variety of people. _____

3 Role play 1 is for two speakers.

A works in recruitment at Random and is interviewing Nicole Pelissier (B) for the
job of Buyer/Planner in Exercise 1.

A looks at this page. B turns to page 78.

B turns to page 78.

SPEAKER A

Role play 1

Use this CV as a basis for the interview, and ask about the points mentioned below.

Nicole Pelissier
1998–present **Nissan Car Plant, Sunderland, UK. Component Buyer**
Negotiate terms for supply of car components, including work on programmes for just-in-time delivery and continuous cost reduction. Report to senior management on progress in these areas. Work with engineers on quality control and delivery schedules.
1990–98 **Renault plant, Lens, Belgium. Assistant Buyer**
Helped Buying Manager in planning component orders, contacts with suppliers, etc. Supervised computer analysis of buying costs.
1987–90 **HEC (Hautes Etudes Commerciales), Paris**
Full-time business qualification.
1979–85 **Lycée Charlemagne, Paris**
Baccalauréat C: Maths specialisation.

Good interpersonal skills   Good computer skills

Interests: Chess, golf and computer games, especially chess and golf simulations

– why does she want to leave job in Newcastle?
– how easy to change from car industry to semiconductors?
– why did she leave job in Lens?
– will she adapt to life in Ireland?
– interpersonal skills?
– when able to start?

Role play 2 is for two speakers.

Change roles. This time, A is interviewing Leslie MacFadden (B) for the job of
Training Manager in Exercise 1.

A looks at this page. B turns to page 78.

SPEAKER A

Role play 2

Use this CV as a basis for the interview, and ask about the points mentioned below.

Leslie MacFadden
1993–present **Trainer, Bell PCs, Dublin**
One of team of seven trainers at Bell assembly plant. Planning and scheduling of wide range of management and technical courses. Responsible to the Head of Training for quality control and analysis of course outcomes.
1987–93 **Physics teacher, Galway High School**
Gave physics lessons at all levels of school, including leaving certificate level.
1986–87 **University College, Galway**
Trained to teach physics in secondary schools.
1983–86 **Midwestern University, Chicago**
Degree in physics.
1981–83 **Lakeside High School, Chicago**

Good interpersonal skills with all levels of employees and management

Interests: baseball, Irish football (amateur player), folk guitar

– family background?
– why does he want this job?
– can he easily adapt to change?
– why did he leave teaching?
– any disputes with colleagues, trainees?
– how does he follow US baseball?
– who does he play football for?

KEY VOCABULARY

Workplaces

Complete these words relating to different parts of a workplace. The first one has been done for you.

1 A place where employees can leave young children while they work:
C R E C H E

2 A place where employees can eat: __ __ N __ __ __ __

3 The place where visitors go when they first arrive: R __ __ __ P __ __ __ __

4 A building or part of a building where work is carried out on new techniques and products: RESEARCH AND DEVELOPMENT L __ B __ __ __ __ T __ __ __

5 A building where things are made: MANUFACTURING P __ __ __ __

6 A place where employees are taught new working methods and skills:
__ R __ __ N __ __ __ CENTRE

7 A place where employees can get exercise: G __ __

1 🎧 The Random plant has been completed and is now working. These recordings were made around the site near the signs shown below. Match each section of the recording (A–F) with the sign that it relates to.

1 ____

2 ____

3 ____ NO TRESPASSING

4 ____ NO ENTRY TO UNAUTHORISED PERSONNEL

5 ____ VISITORS PLEASE REPORT TO RECEPTION ON ARRIVAL

6 ____ ALL DELIVERIES TO GATE 6

2 🎧 You are on a guided tour of the Random plant for potential employees of the company. Listen to the tour commentary, and mark the order in which these places are visited.

____ canteen

____ company gym

____ packing area

____ production area

____ reception area

____ research and development laboratories

____ training centre

3 Now listen to the recording again and choose the correct alternative to answer the questions.

    1 The plant was finished _____.
       a) before the planned date   b) on the planned date
       c) after the planned date

    2 The plant cost _____.
       a) more than planned   b) the amount that had been planned
       c) less than planned

    3 Which product containing chips does the guide *not* mention?
       a) mobile phones   b) television sets   c) cars

    4 About how many people work in the R and D laboratories?
       a) 40   b) 50   c) 60

    5 The work in the R and D laboratories is _____.
       a) secret   b) published on the internet
       c) published in the specialised press

    6 How much do employees pay to use the company gym?
       a) nothing   b) £50 a year   c) £100 a year

    7 The training centre will train _____.
       a) most people who join the company
       b) just some of the people who join the company
       c) just people with no qualifications

    8 In production, the guide says that there have been _____.
       a) so many problems that production has not started
       b) some problems   c) no problems at all

    9 The finished chips are taken from the plant by _____.
       a) trains   b) lorries   c) vans

   10 The tour ends _____.
       a) back in reception   b) in the canteen   c) in the gym

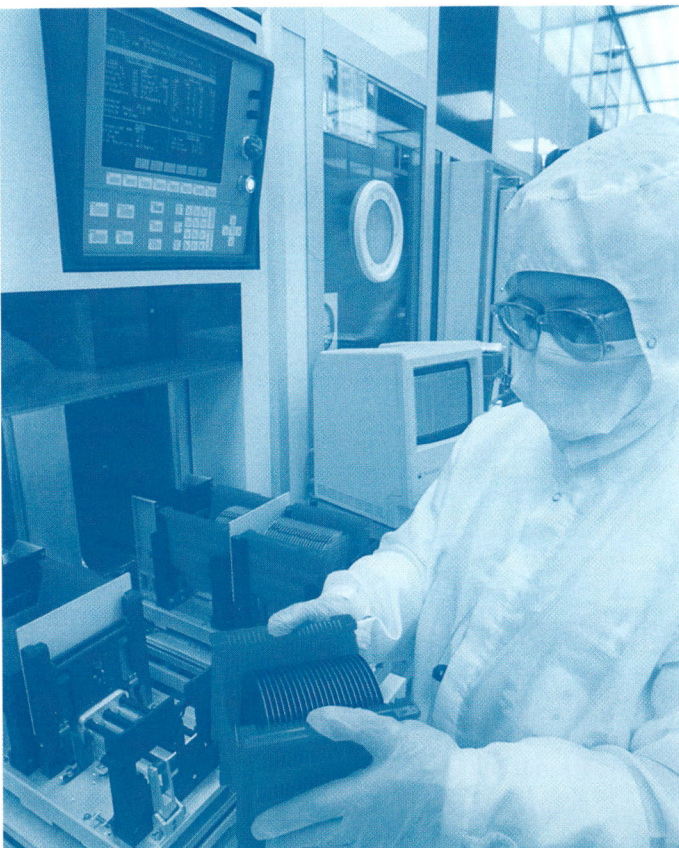

giving opinions

entrepreneurs

exchanging information

UNIT 5

Competition

KEY VOCABULARY

Competition

Match the expressions on the left with the definitions on the right.

1 cartel
2 competition
3 deregulation
4 level playing field
5 market leader
6 monopoly
7 privatisation

A the company or one of the companies that has the highest sales in a particular market
B when companies who should normally be competing agree to fix prices
C when a government sells companies that it owns to investors
D when companies are trying to sell more, be more profitable, etc than other companies
E a situation where there is only one company offering goods or services in a particular market, and it is therefore able to charge what it wants to
F used to talk about a competitive situation which is fair
G relaxing the rules for competition in a particular industry and encouraging competition

A Listening

1 🎧 Here is a list of travellers being interviewed at an airport about a new airline. Listen to the recording and give the order in which they speak.

____ businesswoman   ____ executive from a large company

____ student   ____ self-employed business consultant

____ retired woman   ____ unemployed man

2 Now listen to the recording again and complete the information in the table. If a particular piece of information is not given, write NG in the space in the table.

Traveller	Place come from/going to	Reason for trip	Fare paid	Satisfaction level*
Unemployed man				
Businesswoman				
Executive				
Student				
Business consultant				
Retired woman				

*(10 = extremely satisfied, 0 = extremely dissatisfied)

3 🎧 Listen to this interview from a business programme on the radio. Which of expressions 1–7 in the *Key vocabulary* section above (or related expressions) do you hear?

28

4 Listen to the interview again and choose the correct alternatives to answer the questions.

1 What is the name of Guerrero's airline?
a) Flyway   b) Flyhigh   c) Flyaway

2 What criticism does he *not* make of national airlines?
a) They are run for the benefit of employees rather than passengers.
b) They still consider that flying should be an expensive luxury.
c) They do not have a good safety record.

3 Which of these qualities does he refer to in talking about his own airline?
a) good food   b) punctuality   c) smart uniforms for staff

4 Which of these methods of keeping costs low does he mention?
a) no luxury offices   b) using a different type of plane for each route
c) serving cheap hot meals on the flights

5 What advantage of using a small airport does he *not* mention?
a) Passengers can walk quickly to the plane.
b) There are fewer delays because there is only one big airline using the airport.
c) The charges are less than at other airports.

6 Guerrero is buying a new plane each _____.
a) week   b) month   c) quarter

7 How many airlines does Guerrero think there will be in ten years?
a) twice as many   b) three times as many
c) He doesn't give an exact figure

8 How many planes, routes and staff did the airline have five years ago?
a) two planes, two routes and 40 staff
b) two planes, three routes and 50 staff
c) three planes, three routes and 60 staff

9 How many routes and staff does it have now?
a) 50 routes and 500 staff   b) 15 routes and 900 staff
c) 55 routes and 800 staff

10 What is Guerrero's ambition for the airline in ten years' time?
a) to be a market leader in European air travel
b) to be *the* market leader in European air travel
c) to eliminate all national airlines

KEY VOCABULARY
Entrepreneurs

Complete the commentary using the expressions in the box.

venture capitalists	start-ups	hi-tech	entrepreneur	growth

Someone who is willing to take the risk of starting a business from nothing is an (1) _____. The related adjective is *entrepreneurial*, and the quality that entrepreneurs possess is *entrepreneurship*. Entrepreneurs often start businesses in new areas based on advanced technologies: their businesses are (2) _____. Entrepreneurs sometimes get the money they need to start their business from (3) _____. These are individuals or financial institutions that invest in (4) _____ knowing that most will fail, but that they will make a lot of money with the ones that succeed.

An entrepreneur may sell their company once it becomes successful, often to a larger company. Some entrepreneurial people prefer to do this, rather than stay and manage an "ordinary" successful company, something they may find less exciting than the period of fast (5) _____ when the company is new.

KEY QUESTIONS
Start-ups

Match the two parts of these questions that you could ask about entrepreneurs.

1	What's Arturo's	before starting her company?
2	When did Belinda	do/make?
3	Where did Carlos	the company based?
4	What had Dagmar done	get the finance to start his company?
5	What does the company	start her company?
6	Where is	of the company now?
7	What is the value	background?

KEY ANSWERS
Start-ups

Now match the questions above with these answers.

a) She had worked in a lot of different companies, but had always wanted to be her own boss.
b) It's worth ten million euros.
c) She founded the company five years ago, but she'd been wanting to do it for a long time before that.
d) It has its main office in Lisbon, with another in Porto.
e) He has a background in journalism. He did a degree in literature, a master's in media studies and then worked on a national paper for ten years.
f) It designs software for special applications.
g) He contacted a lot of banks, but they weren't interested, so he went to a firm of venture capitalists.

1 This role play is for two speakers.

A and B are journalists who want to write an article about entrepreneurs.

A knows more than B about some of the entrepreneurs, and B knows more than A about the others.

Each gets information from the other to complete the information they already have.

A looks at this page. B turns to page 79.

SPEAKER A

Entrepreneur	Name of company and base	Product or or service	History
Francisco Guerrero	Flyaway, Croydon Airport, near London, UK	Air travel	Founded Flyaway in 1995, with money from his father's hotel business in Spain. Started with two planes, just two routes and 40 staff. Today, more than 900 staff and four million passengers a year on 15 routes.
_____ _____	Aston Molecules, Aston Science Park, near Aston University, UK	_____ _____	Slack was a university teacher of _____. Bought the business from its founder, Malcolm Stevens, another university teacher, in _____. Slack _____ the company in 1996 to US drugs firm OSI, but remained as Managing Director.
William Son	NeoPoint, San Diego, California	Information services	Son graduated from the University of California in San Diego. Worked for Qualcomm in Korea before founding NeoPoint in 1997, developing smart (intelligent) phones and information services. Emerging Entrepreneur of the Year Award, 1999.
_____ _____	_____ _____ _____	oil refining	After the fall of communism, _____ was the first person to register a private company in the country. An _____ by training, he got into the property business _____. Now one of the richest people in Romania.
Gisele Rufer	Delance, Macolin, Switzerland	Watches for women	Rufer worked as a designer in a large watch company. Asked to produce designs for women's watches, the designs were not accepted by the company's male-dominated management, so she left and set up her own company with her business partner, Carol Gygax.
_____ _____ _____	_____ _____	_____ _____ for buying everything from flights to babysitting services	_____, son of Wall Street banker. _____, daughter of Oxford history professor. _____'s father told him business plan would not work. Company now worth several hundred million pounds _____.

C   Reading and writing

1 Read this article and complete the tasks.

EVER THOUGHT OF STARTING YOUR OWN COMPANY? Carla Manzoni is Professor of Entrepreneurship at the University of Croydon's Management Institute. She has recently completed a year-long study of 300 European entrepreneurs, and she has this advice to give to the business leaders of tomorrow.

1 "It sounds obvious, but make sure that you really have something new to offer, in terms of technical innovation, lower prices or both. Half the start-ups I studied went out of business after less than two years, and one of the main reasons for this was that their product or service had no advantages that were not available elsewhere.

2 Allow enough time. All the factors I'm going to mention are extremely time-consuming. You will be impatient to get going, and by nature entrepreneurs are optimists. But most of the people you deal with – potential investors, your team, suppliers, and customers – will have many other demands on their time, even if you think your idea is fantastic.

3 Be realistic about the amount of money you will need. You will probably have to go to several sources of finance. Think of all the things you will have to pay for before you make your first sale: development costs, premises, payment of suppliers, employees' salaries, unforeseen problems. The list is endless.

4 Work on your presentation to potential investors. They may see a dozen or more every day. Make it short and to the point. People won't decide to invest in your idea in the first five minutes, but they will certainly eliminate you in that time if they don't understand your idea very quickly.

5 Choose the right people to work with. It takes time to find the right combination of specialists on the technical side, in marketing and so on. At one point, someone in your team may begin to wonder why they gave up their well-paid job in a big company just to join you. And then a key person may leave at a difficult moment, for example right after the launch.

6 It takes time to build the confidence of suppliers. They have functioning businesses, but all you have is an idea. You may have to negotiate special payment terms with them. Your business plan should be realistic about when they will have to be paid. Delaying payments to suppliers, for example because you started to sell later than you thought you would, will damage your relations with them, and this will cause problems. You will also need to know who your customers are going to be. For example, if you're selling to supermarkets, you'll need to find out who the buyers are for the big chains, and then fix meetings with them. Again, this will take time.

I hope I haven't put you off the idea of starting your own business. The rewards can be tremendous. But it's better to go into it prepared, and realistic about the energy required and the stress involved. Good luck!"

Choose the best title for each numbered paragraph from a–h below. Do not use any letter more than once.

Paragraph 1 _____   Paragraph 4 _____

Paragraph 2 _____   Paragraph 5 _____

Paragraph 3 _____   Paragraph 6 _____

a) Think carefully about suppliers and customers.
b) Think of the effect of not having time for your family.
c) Get the right people to work with.
d) Don't underestimate the amount of money you will need.
e) Think about when you're going to sell your company after you've made a lot of money.
f) Carefully prepare your presentation to the people who are going to put money into your company.
g) Be realistic about the time involved.
h) Be sure you have a really new idea.

2 Using the information in the text, complete each sentence with a phrase from the list below. Do not use any phrase more than once.

1 Carla Manzoni is a professor of management and she _____.
2 In setting up their own business, people often make the mistake of

   _____.

3 In dealing with suppliers, make sure that _____.

a) is against the idea of people setting up their own business
b) they know when they will be paid
c) underestimating how long it will take
d) selling the company too soon
e) has just completed a study of people who set up their own business

3 You are an entrepreneur with a new business idea. You have written to an organisation called NewStart Investments to ask for a meeting to discuss getting finance from them. You receive this e-mail from them.

In most of the numbered lines (1–5) there is one extra word that does not fit. One or two lines are correct, however. If a line is correct, put a tick (✓) against it. If there is an extra word in a line, cross it out.

Sender: Joan Lambert
Date: 8 January
Subject: finance start-up

Thank you for your letter requesting a meeting to discuss start-up
1 finance for your new company. My colleagues and I have studied your as outline   _____
2 business plan and we would be pleased for to see you on Monday 15 January,   _____
3 from 2 to 2.30 pm. Please come to our Broad Street address and ask for me at reception,   _____
4 and I will send someone down for to meet you. You will then have the opportunity   _____
5 to make in a short presentation to myself and my colleague Brian Armstrong.   _____

Looking forward to hearing from you,

All best wishes,

Joan Lambert
NewStart Investments

4 Now write a reply to the e-mail in Exercise 3, including these points. (See page 7 for an example of an e-mail.)

- Thank Joan Lambert for her e-mail.
- Say that you cannot meet her on 15 January, as you have an important meeting with a potentially important customer that day (a supermarket chain).
- Ask her for a meeting any other day during the week beginning 15 January.
- Apologise.
- Close appropriately.

the working environment

dealing with figures

suppliers, wholesalers and retailers

Better ways of working

Ways of working

Combine the words on the left with the words on the right to form compounds that match definitions a–f below.

1	self-employed	computer
2	office	network
3	laptop	person
4	home	furniture
5	computer	machine
6	coffee	working

a) a small computer that you can carry with you easily

b) someone who works for one or more client companies, rather than as a company employee

c) desks, tables, etc of the kind you often see in companies

d) what b) often does

e) the system that allows all the computers in an organisation to work together

f) the place in a company where you often find out things first

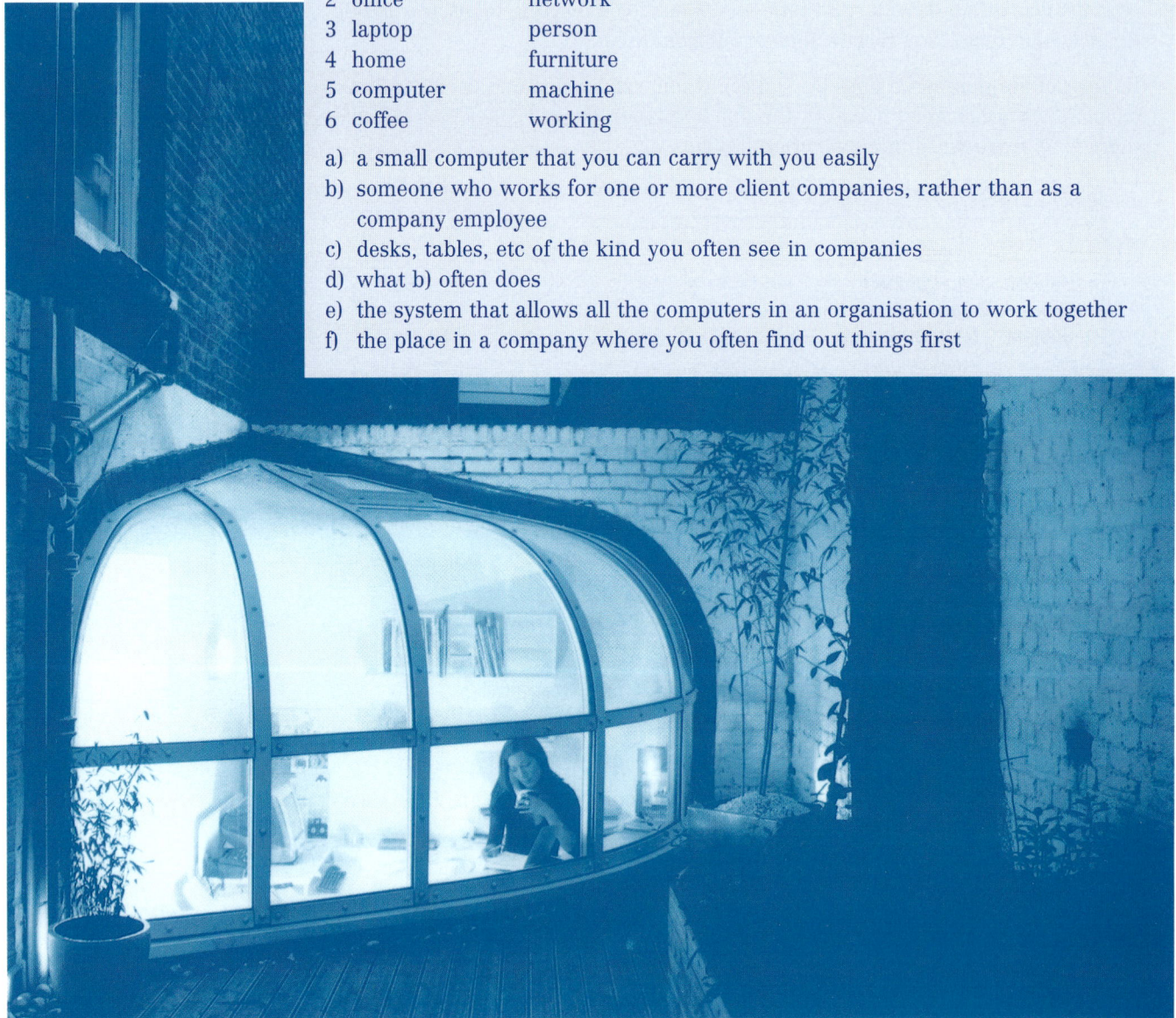

A ## Listening

1   Listen to six people talking about where they work and what they work on. Give the order in which they speak.

____ head of large company   ____ office manager

____ self-employed person   ____ secretary

____ advertising executive   ____ salesperson

2 🎧 Matthew Rawlinson is a consultant to companies on ways of improving the working environment of their employees. Listen to what he says and choose the correct alternatives to answer the questions.

1 He says that the design of modern office buildings _____.
   a) can look good from the outside and be good for people working in them
   b) can look good from the outside but be bad for the people working in them
   c) can look bad from the outside and be bad for people working in them

2 Modern office lighting _____.
   a) can be very restful for your eyes
   b) can be very tiring for your eyes
   c) has no effect on your eyes

3 When you correctly adjust the brightness of your computer screen, you

   _____.
   a) can safely use your computer continuously all day
   b) can use your computer for an hour every day
   c) should still take regular breaks from using your computer if you can

4 The best way to sit when using a computer is to _____.
   a) sit upright with your feet just touching the floor
   b) sit upright with the weight of your thighs on your feet
   c) sit back with your entire weight on the back of the chair

5 What does Matthew Rawlinson *not* mention as one of the disadvantages of working in an open-plan office?
   a) It's not possible to have private telephone conversations.
   b) People interrupt you to ask about things that are not your responsibility.
   c) Working surrounded by other people can be difficult.

6 What word does he use that means the same as home working?
   a) telecommuting   b) teleworking   c) teletyping

7 What reason does he give for some managers not accepting home working?
   a) They don't like the idea of empty offices for which the company is paying rent.
   b) They prefer to see the people they manage.
   c) They think their employees will be lazy.

8 Does he think that home working will become more popular?
   a) yes   b) no   c) perhaps

9 Matthew thinks that, ideally, people working from home should work

   _____.
   a) anywhere that is suitable
   b) where they can keep an eye on their children
   c) in a suitably equipped room

10 He thinks that a good way of keeping work and family life separate is to

   _____.
   a) forbid anyone else to use your computer in the evening
   b) close the door of the room where you work when you finish in the evening
   c) persuade your partner to work at home as well

KEY VOCABULARY
Ordering things

Put these events in order to give two mini-scenarios, one where things go right and one where things go wrong. The first four steps are the same for both scenarios.

a) A week later, the goods finally arrive. Some of the goods have been **damaged in transit**. Others have manufacturing **flaws** or **defects**. You are not pleased.

b) Someone takes your order and gives you the **delivery date**.

c) The delivery date comes, but nothing arrives. You phone to ask where your goods are. You are told that your goods have been **delayed**. It turns out they have been delivered to the wrong place.

d) The goods arrive on the delivery date. Everything is perfect. You are very pleased.

e) You phone again, this time to **order** it or to **place an order**.

f) You phone to find out more about it: whether the thing you want is **in stock** and **available** immediately or whether you have to wait. You want to know if there's a **discount** if you buy **in bulk** (if you buy several).

g) You see something you like in a **catalogue**.

Scenario 1	Scenario 2
1 _____	1 _____
2 _____	2 _____
3 _____	3 _____
4 _____	4 _____
5 _____	5 _____
	6 _____

KEY QUESTIONS AND ANSWERS
Ordering things

Match the questions on the left with the answers on the right.

1 What is this chair made of?

2 What's the difference between the two models?

3 How much does this model cost?

4 What are the payment terms for the first order?

5 Is it possible for companies to open an account?

6 Is there a discount for bulk orders?

7 How much do you charge for delivery?

8 How soon can you deliver?

A Two hundred euros including VAT.

B Leather.

C This model is made of leather and that one is made of plastic.

D Delivery is ten euros for orders under 100 euros and free for orders of 100 euros or more.

E We ask for payment before delivery for the first order.

F After the first order, you can open an account.

G If you place your order before 12 noon, we normally deliver the next working day.

H If you order more than ten of the same item, we offer 10% discount.

1 Role play 1 is for two speakers.

A is an office manager and wants to order a number of office chairs.

B works in the call centre of Office Planet, a company that specialises in selling office equipment by telephone.

A phones B to get more information about the chairs in Office Planet's catalogue.

A looks at this page. B turns to page 80.

SPEAKER A

Role play 1

Exec	Sten	Soho
Leather covering Available in black or brown Price: 295 euros	Covering looks like leather Available in black Price: 85 euros	Nylon covering Available in red, blue or green Price: 50 euros

You want to order 75 chairs for your staff. You are hesitating between Sten and Soho. Ask:
• if Sten is only available in black
• what the covering is really made of, whether it's long-lasting, etc
• what the differences are between Sten and Soho
• what the delivery date is for each type of chair
• what the discount is if you order 75: you think 20% would be reasonable

You also want an Exec chair for yourself. Ask:
• if it's real leather
• whether there are other colours available
• what the delivery date is
• whether you can have an Exec chair at a greatly reduced price (30% off?) if you order 75 Sten or Soho chairs.

Role play 2 is for two speakers.

The next day, B phones A. A looks at this page. B turns to page 80 again.

SPEAKER A

Role play 2

• Ask if B has spoken to their boss about a bigger discount on the Exec if you order 75 Sten or Soho model chairs.
• If there is a bigger discount, place a firm order for 75 Sten or Soho model chairs (you choose) and give details for delivery: invent the details or give your own company's name and address.
• Ask when you will receive your Exec.
• Ask if you can open an account, as you are a trade customer. What are the payment terms?

Reading and writing

Makers, sellers and buyers

When someone describes products or services, they may talk about:

1 companies that are **makers** or **manufacturers** of goods, or **providers** of services

2 **distributors** or **wholesalers**: organisations that sell the products of many manufacturers to other **sellers**, for example **retailers** selling to the public

3 **buyers** of goods or services: **customers** in the case of goods and some services like banking services, and **clients** of other services such as those of lawyers or advertising agencies

4 companies that sell to other companies **business-to-business (B2B)**

5 people that buy for themselves and their families: **consumers**, especially when considered as part of large groups of such people

1 Talk briefly about the company you work for (or one you would like to work for) and the products it makes or sells, or the services it provides, using the points above. Then make notes while other members of the group do the same. Find similarities and differences between the companies.

2 Read this article from a business magazine and complete the tasks.

GOOD FURNITURE BY DESIGN

① Meblopol is one of a new breed of Polish companies. It was founded in 1993 by Anna Nowak and Ewa Kowalska. Anna and Ewa had been students together at art school. Anna takes up the story. "Ewa and I were both very interested in furniture during our time as students. It was a very practical course, not just theory. We looked not only at design but at the suitability of different materials for different manufacturing processes. We visited a lot of small workshops making furniture, saw how they were doing things and thought about ways of improving their methods."

② Ewa says that another factor in their success was carefully studying the market and existing products. "We looked at design magazines and furniture catalogues from all over Europe and the United States. It seemed to us that a lot of office furniture was very dull and unimaginative. Even at work, especially at work, perhaps, people want an environment that is light and cheerful. It depends on the company of course, but in a lot of places, people want their workplaces to be fun to be in. There's no reason why everything has to be black or grey."

③ So with a bank loan, Anna and Ewa started production in a garage in the suburbs of Warsaw. "Things were very difficult at first," recalls Anna. "We had a few small orders from furniture shops in Poland, but the bigger clients are much more difficult to find. It is hard getting meetings with the key decision-makers, the buyers."

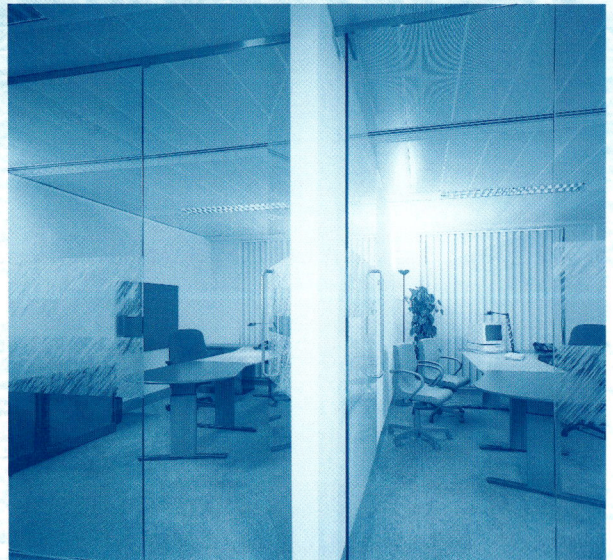

④ "Each country has its key distributors, and it is important to find out how the market in each place works," says Anna. "We have started to develop sales with national chains outside Poland, but it can be very hard work. I go on a lot of trips but often come back with nothing much to show for them. But I know that these trips are essential if I'm going to get business. And these trips are beginning to pay off. Recently we've started to make progress in western Europe. I've made some very interesting contacts in Italy, and we are also working hard on France and Spain. It's a question of persevering until something happens."

Choose the best one-sentence summary for each paragraph of the article from this list. Write the number of the paragraph next to each summary. If a summary is not used, put a cross (✗).

a) The history of Polish furniture design. _____

b) Studying markets and existing products. _____

c) Starting production and getting the first orders. _____

d) How the big furniture chains operate. _____

e) Getting into new markets is hard work and involves a lot of travelling. _____

f) Furniture manufacturing in different countries. _____

g) Anna Nowak and Ewa Kowalska start up their furniture business. _____

3 Choose the correct alternative to complete the sentences from a–h below.

1 While they were students, Anna and Ewa visited small furniture workshops in order to _____.

2 They decided what to make and offer to customers by _____.

3 In the first few years after they founded Meblopol _____.

4 Anna and Ewa wanted to sell more to _____.

5 Meblopol has begun to do business with companies _____.

6 Meblopol has now built a large plant and _____.

a) in western Europe
b) within Poland
c) study their methods
d) business was slow
e) national chains outside Poland
f) has plans to expand it next year
g) studying the market and existing products
h) copy their methods and their products

4 Imagine a letter that Ewa Kowalska writes to an Italian furniture wholesalers in Milan called DMI, trying to get a meeting with them. She knows that their chief buyer's name is Giuseppe Roselli. Write a letter to him including the points and the phrases below.

Open appropriately
   Dear ...

Mention that you saw DMI featured in a trade magazine
   I saw your company featured in a trade magazine and ...

Give a brief outline of Meblopol's history (2 sentences)
   I am the co-founder of a company based in Warsaw called Meblopol ...

Say that you want to expand and would like to start selling your products in southern Europe, especially Italy
   We are hoping to expand further and would like to ...

Say that you will be in Italy next week and that you could come to Milan on Thursday or Friday
   I will be in Italy next week. Would it be possible to ...

Say that you are enclosing a copy of your current catalogue
   I'm enclosing a copy of our current catalogue so that ...

Close appropriately
   Looking forward to ...

Going for growth

lending and borrowing money

negotiating a loan

complaining about poor performance

Growth

Complete the commentary using the words in the box.

boom	boom and bust	grew	takes off
growth	grown	levels off	

If a business increases its activity, it *grows*. The past tense of this verb is

(1) _____ and the past participle is (2) _____. The

corresponding noun is (3) _____. If an activity starts growing very

fast for the first time, it (4) _____.

If a business is growing fast, it is *booming*. The corresponding noun is

(5) _____. When an activity stops growing, but does not fall, it

(6) _____.

A period of fast growth followed by a period when the amount of activity

falls is one of (7) _____.

A ## Reading and writing

1 ◄UNIT 1► Read this article from the *Australian Franchising Bulletin*, and mark
the statements on page 41 true or false.

> THE AUSTRALIAN FRANCHISE FEDERATION (AFF) today unveiled a new survey that
> confirms a continuing boom in the franchising sector over the past year.
>
> The federation's annual survey of franchised businesses shows the sector
> continued to grow at 15 per cent, a level that has continued since the end of the last
> recession in the early 1990s. The federation's chairman, Bill Hawke, said, "These are
> encouraging figures. The outlook for the franchising business is very healthy."
> There are believed to be more than 300 franchise systems in Australia, including
> some big global names.
>
> The report shows that the most popular businesses for franchising continue to be
> retail outlets. However, other service businesses are also showing strong growth.
> One area the federation thinks is likely to take off over the next few years is
> property and building services. The survey also shows that the cost of getting into
> a franchise is dropping. The average start-up cost for a franchise is believed to be
> about A$120,000 – down from A$135,000 last year.
>
> Business consultant Francine Gordon says that many small business owners lack
> basic management and business skills. Gordon is the author of *Franchising without
> Tears*. She says that most independent small business owners do not understand the
> basic functioning of a business. Gordon says that seven out of ten small businesses
> fail within five years. "With franchising, the risks of failure are lower, because a
> good franchise can provide a strong basic business model for franchisees to follow,"
> she says. "A franchise is not a guarantee of success, but it certainly helps."

1 The AFF published its survey some time ago.   T   F
2 The boom in franchising in Australia has just started.   T   F
3 Franchising is growing at 15% per year.   T   F
4 The chairman of the AFF is satisfied with the growth in franchising
   in Australia.   T   F
5 The franchises in Australia are all of Australian origin.   T   F
6 Shops are the most popular forms of franchise at the moment.   T   F
7 Shops will continue to be the only real areas of growth in franchising.   T   F
8 To open a franchise now, you need at least A$135,000.   T   F
9 According to Gordon, most independent small businesses fail
   because they do not sell enough.   T   F
10 It's less probable that a franchise will go out of business than an
   independent company.   T   F

2 Read this advertisement from the *Australian Franchising Bulletin* and complete
the task.

❶ _____

SMART Kitchens caters for the home kitchen market, constructing kitchens from basic models right up to complex installations with the latest equipment from the US and Europe. Established in 1979, it has a proven record, having successfully installed more than 50,000 kitchens. The franchise system provides the strength and efficiency for design and production with high quality and service. Franchisees will be qualified builders, carpenters, etc, and need to be friendly and outgoing.

There are 30 franchises in Australia and eight in New Zealand, with plans for further expansion.

❷ _____

Capital required: A$150,000
Fees: A$1,000/month
Advertising charge: cities – A$3,000/month;
  country – A$1,500/month
Target turnover: cities – A$100–150,000/month;
  country – A$70,000–100,000/month

❸ _____

Includes initial and ongoing training, marketing support, group advertising, group buying, and technical and management back-up.

❹ _____

Rebecca Harris,
Smart Kitchens Pty Ltd,
1 Canberra Parade,
Oakleigh, Melbourne,
Victoria 3012

Telephone: (03) 9325 7300
Fax: (03) 9325 7350
E-mail: rebecca.harris@smartkitchens.com

For 1–4 above, choose the best title from a–g below.

a) The chances of success   e) Legal issues
b) Contact   f) Our franchise system
c) Franchisor support   g) Boom and bust
d) Financial aspects

3 Using the information in brackets, write an e-mail to Rebecca Harris at Smart Kitchens saying that you would like to become one of their franchisees. Say:

- where you want to open the franchise (Darwin)
- how much business experience you have (three years as an independent installer with two employees)
- how much kitchen-building experience you have (ten years as an installer working for someone else before you started your own business three years ago)
- how much capital you have (A$50,000). You want to know if this is enough.

Ask her to phone you to discuss the possibilities – your number is Darwin (08) 3452 8934. Close appropriately.

B Speaking

KEY VOCABULARY

Lending

Match the expressions on the left with the definitions on the right.

1	principal	A	the amount you pay to the lender for a loan
2	interest	B	the main part of a loan
3	security or collateral	C	to fail to make repayments
4	default	D	the percentage at which interest is charged
5	interest rate	E	a type of loan made by a bank when you spend more money than you have in your bank account
6	overdraft	F	something the lender can take and sell if you do not make repayments

1 Role play 1 is for two speakers.

A is Rebecca Harris, the person from Smart Kitchens who deals with new franchisees.

B is interested in becoming a franchisee of Smart Kitchens.

A looks at this page. B turns to page 81.

SPEAKER A

Role play 1

Phone B to get more details about the information B sent in their e-mail. Start by thanking B for their e-mail, and then use the notes below as a basis for your questions.

3 years as an independent installer with 2 employees
Successful? Sales per year? Who were employees? Will they continue?
10 years as an installer working for someone else before you started your own business 3 years ago
Why take franchise now? Not successful? (Be tactful about this.)
A$50,000 capital
Not enough. A$150,000 minimum. Possible to get bank loan?

You have another question:
Like dealing with people? Friendly?

Close the conversation politely and ask B to get back in touch when they have enough capital.

Role play 2 is for two speakers.

A works at a bank on loan applications.

After the conversation with Rebecca Harris, B goes to their bank to ask for a loan in order to start a franchise.

A looks at this page. B turns to page 81.

SPEAKER A

Role play 2

After some small talk, ask B:
- about their background in the kitchen installing business
- who they intend to work with
- how much capital they require and what they need it for
- what the probable turnover will be and if this is realistic
- how much capital they already have
- if they can offer anything as security, such as their house

End the conversation by saying that you will consider the application and will be back in touch soon.

Role play 3 is for two speakers.

A few days later, A phones B with a decision.

A looks at this page. B turns to page 81.

SPEAKER A

Role play 3

Use these notes to explain your decision.
- you have checked the Smart Kitchens franchise system – seems to be OK
- you have seen their advertising – have even thought about getting one installed yourself!
- you can approve loan of A$100,000, but over three years rather than five
- loan to be secured on B's house – if B cannot make repayments, bank has the right to take and sell B's house. B understands and accepts this?

End the conversation by saying that B can think about the offer and let the bank know in a few days.

C Listening

Unjustified complaints

Look again at the language of complaints on page 8. Now look at these expressions for replying politely to complaints that are unjustified.

a) I think there's been a misunderstanding.
b) If you take a closer look, I think you'll find that ...
c) Try turning it down a bit.
d) If you look in the instruction manual, you'll see the required settings.
e) Are you sure it's connected OK?

You can respond by saying:
My mistake. I didn't ...
OK. I see now. I didn't realise you had to ...
Oh right. I didn't know about that.
OK. I've got it now. I didn't understand ...
I see. If all else fails, read the instructions!

1 Listen to the complaints from customers of one of Smart Kitchens' franchisees. Which of the first group of expressions above (a–e) do you hear in each conversation? One of the conversations does not contain any of the expressions. Show this by putting a cross (✗) next to the conversation.

1 _____   3 _____   5 _____

2 _____   4 _____

2 Now listen to the recording again. Below are some possible continuations of the conversations. Which continuation goes with which conversation?

a) Yes, but your quote could have been clearer, all on one page. If I'd known it was going to be this expensive, I wouldn't have had a new kitchen in the first place. _____

b) Oh right. I didn't know about that. I thought the guys who did the installation took the old stuff away as well. _____

c) My mistake. How stupid of me. I'm always getting mixed up with dates. Sorry about that. _____

d) Right. I didn't know about that. I'll go and look at it now. I seem to remember the switch being mentioned in the instructions for use. _____

e) I see. Same old story. If all else fails, read the instructions! I'm glad about that: I don't like cold beer! _____

3 Listen to this interview with a bank executive talking about how their bank decides which small businesses to give loans to. Which of the expressions below occur in the interview?

a) loans	h) business plan
b) accounts	i) sales
c) cheques	j) revenue
d) personal finances	k) debts
e) amounts	l) costs
f) overdrafts	m) repayments
g) strategy	n) profit

4 Now listen to the recording again and choose the correct alternative to answer the questions.

1 How many years has this bank executive dealt with loans?
   a) three   b) five   c) ten

2 In deciding whether to make a loan to an existing client, which of these things does the speaker *not* mention?
   a) personal contact   b) the type of business they are in   c) overdrafts

3 If you start a business from scratch, does the business already exist?
   a) yes   b) no   c) sometimes

4 The speaker mentions the personal finances of people asking for business loans because _____.
   a) the bank may want to ask them to use their own money to repay the loan
   b) someone's personal finances are a good guide to how they will run a business
   c) if they have enough money themselves, they shouldn't need a loan

5 In deciding whether to give a loan, the most important thing is the _____.
   a) business plan   b) type of business   c) attitude of the borrower

6 When asked what they mean by "realistic", the speaker says, "That's the $64,000 question." By this, the speaker means that _____.
   a) someone has asked for a loan of $64,000
   b) $64,000 is the maximum that the bank will lend
   c) it's a very important question, but a difficult one to answer

7 In deciding if a business plan is realistic, the bank analyses _____.
   a) probable sales and costs for the business
   b) research into the type of business the loan is for
   c) the probable future direction of the economy as a whole

8 The last question asked by the interviewer is about _____.
   a) the attitudes of banks to lending to small businesses
   b) the idea that lending is limited by general economic growth
   c) banks' attitudes to types of business they don't know anything about

9 The bank executive says that banks have to be careful about lending because _____.
   a) of government regulations
   b) they want to limit the number of bad loans
   c) banks don't like lending to small businesses

10 The speaker says that banks are not charities. Charities are _____.
   a) government departments
   b) small businesses
   c) organisations whose purpose is to help people, bring benefits to society, etc, rather than to make a profit

UNIT 8

Projects and schedules

KEY EXPRESSIONS

Arrival and greetings

Match the expressions on the left with the appropriate responses on the right.

1 Very nice to meet you.
2 Did you have a good flight?
3 Would you like some coffee?
4 Take a seat.
5 How's your hotel?
6 The weather's not too good, I'm afraid.
7 Let's go up to my office.

A No problem. It's very good to be here, anyway.
B Right.
C Comfortable and very quiet.
D Everything went very smoothly. No delays anywhere.
E Good to meet *you*.
F Please.
G Thanks.

A Listening and speaking

1 🎧 ◀UNIT 2▶ Alvin Palmer, Chief Executive of GCDC (Golf Course Design and Construction Inc), and Jerry Salinas, its Technical Director, are in Crete to discuss the construction of a golf course with Stavros Milatos, head of the Crete Hoteliers' Association. Palmer and Salinas have arrived at Milatos's office.

Listen to their conversation and say which of the above expressions (1–7) you do *not* hear.

KEY VOCABULARY

Schedules

Complete the commentary using the expressions in the box.

> ahead of schedule   behind schedule   completion   delayed
> lead-time   parallel   phases   schedule   stages

A project usually consists of a number of (1) _____ or
(2) _____. Some can run in (3) _____: they can be done
at the same time. Other stages have to be completed before the next one can
begin. The (4) _____ gives the dates for the (5) _____
of the different stages. If a stage is finished early, the project is
(6) _____, and if it is finished late, the project is
(7) _____ or (8) _____. The length of a
project, or of a particular stage, is its (9) _____.

2 Listen to extracts 1–5 and say which person is speaking in each one.

airline pilot ____

author ____

banker ____

building engineer ____

computer programmer ____

doctor ____

teacher ____

3 Listen to Jerry Salinas discussing the golf course project with Stavros Milatos
and complete the diagram showing its different stages. The first two stages are
already shown on the diagram. (It is now November.)

1 get estimates from local building firms
2 finalise plans
3 install pipes for watering grass
4 undertake main construction of course
5 lay grass
6 carry out construction of buildings, etc
7 add finishing touches
8 open the course

Dec	Jan	Feb	Mar	Apr	May	June	July	Aug	Sept	Oct	Nov
a *1*		c	e							g	h
b *2*		d							f		

4 Now use the complete chart to make a short presentation about the different
stages of the construction of the golf course.

KEY VOCABULARY

Budgets

Complete the commentary using the expressions in the box.

| income | over budget | overrun | overspend |
| spending | under budget | underspend |

A budget is a plan for (1) _____ on a particular project or activity.
It shows how the money is going to be spent and may also include details of
(2) _____, money that the project is going to earn. If you spend less
than planned on a particular project, you (3) _____ and the project
comes in (4) _____. If you spend more, you
(5) _____, it comes in (6) _____ and there
is a cost (7) _____.

1 Read this article from the English-language *Crete Daily News* and choose the correct alternative to fill each gap.

GOLF COURSE OPENS AHEAD OF SCHEDULE

THERE WERE celebrations in Khania as its first golf course opened today, one month ahead of schedule.

In a speech at the opening (1) _____, Stavros Milatos, head of the Crete Hoteliers' Association, paid tribute to the "close (2) _____" with Golf Course Design and Construction Inc, the American builders of the project. "We have had very friendly dealings with GCDC," said Mr Milatos. "They have worked very closely with local (3) _____ companies, and this collaboration has meant that we are able to open the course a month earlier than originally planned, 10 per cent under (4) _____: an amazing achievement."

Mr Milatos was joined at the ceremony by Alvin Palmer, head of GCDC. "It's been a great (5) _____ working on this project," said Mr Palmer. "The site is (6) _____: golf courses next to the sea have something special about them."

Mr Milatos and Mr Palmer were joined as the first players on the course by Spiros Kanaris, mayor of Khania, who said afterwards, "We are very fortunate to have these new (7) _____ on our doorstep. The course will help make the tourist industry here an all-year-round business."

Comments from visitors were equally (8) _____. "This is one of the most beautiful courses I've played on," said Bernhard Braun from Hamburg. "I'll certainly be coming down here again during the winter. They tell me there are a lot of sunny winter days with temperatures of 20 to 25 degrees." On the course there were also visitors from Scandinavia, France, Britain and Ireland. They had a lot of (9) _____ for the facilities. Comments ranged from "a scenic, but technically (10) _____ course" (Pascale Giroud, Versailles), to the "best clubhouse bar this side of Galway" (Liam O'Connor, Dublin).

(11) _____ are already under way for further golf courses on Crete. Sites under consideration include one near Heraklion, and another in the south of the island, near the resort of Ierapetra. Mr Milatos said, "We are in close (12) _____ with colleagues in other parts of the island. Of course, they will be watching developments here closely, but all the initial signs here are that the Khania course is going to be a very successful project."

1	a) ceremony	b) ceremonial	c) meeting	d) ritual
2	a) collaboration	b) collusion	c) competition	d) confrontation
3	a) contraction	b) construction	c) continuation	d) containerisation
4	a) budget	b) costing	c) expenses	d) spending
5	a) prestige	b) pleasing	c) pleased	d) pleasure
6	a) idyll	b) idealistic	c) idealism	d) ideal
7	a) facile	b) facilities	c) facility	d) faculties
8	a) enthusing	b) enthusiastic	c) enthusiasm	d) enthuse
9	a) praise	b) pray	c) prayers	d) prizes
10	a) interest	b) interests	c) interested	d) interesting
11	a) arguments	b) debates	c) discussions	d) discourses
12	a) contacts	b) contract	c) talks	d) touch

2 Are the following statements true or false, according to the article?

1	The golf course opened late.	T	F
2	The golf course cost as much to build as had been planned.	T	F
3	The working relationship between the Crete Hoteliers' Association and GCDC was good.	T	F
4	Alvin Palmer thinks that working on the course was stressful and unpleasant.	T	F
5	The mayor of Khania thinks the course is too far from Khania.	T	F
6	Bernhard Braun intends to visit Crete again during the winter.	T	F
7	Pascale Giroud thinks the course is too easy.	T	F
8	Liam O'Connor likes the facilities.	T	F
9	Other golf courses may be built on Crete in the future.	T	F
10	The writer thinks the Khania course will definitely be a success.	T	F

3 You work for a German tour operator who wants to offer new golf holidays. Write a fax to the Khania Tourist Office, including the following:

- Say that you have heard about the new golf course near Khania from a friend who has been there.
- Ask the tourist office whether there is a brochure about the golf course, and if so, if they can send 5,000 copies.
- Ask about special rates for tour operators who send customers there.
- Ask for 5,000 brochures about Khania in general.
- Ask which hotels are the best ones to stay in for golfers using the course.

Close appropriately.

4 You work for the Khania Tourist Office. Write a fax in reply to the one you have received from a German tour operator, including the following:

- thank the tour operator for inquiry about golf in Khania
- golf course now fully open, and very successful
- you will send 5,000 copies of the golf course brochure today
- for discounts, tour operator to contact golf course directly
- general Khania brochure being reprinted: will send next month when available
- information about hotels on list (next page of this fax)

Close appropriately.

Speaking

KEY QUESTIONS
Location

Here are some ways of talking about where something is:
Is the golf course **far from** Khania?
Is the Athena Hotel **a long way from** the golf course?
Where exactly is the hotel **located/situated**?
Where is the hotel **in relation to** the golf course?
Which is the most **convenient** hotel for the course?

KEY VOCABULARY
Location

The Khania Palace Hotel is in Ayios Marina, **not far from** the centre of the town.
The Athena is in the middle of Khania, **right on** the port.
The Apollo is in a place called Kolimvari, about 25 km **west of** the golf course.
The Helena is (right) **opposite** the entrance to the golf course.
This hotel is very **convenient for** the course. In fact, it's **right next door**.

You are explaining where things are in your town to a potential visitor. With a partner, practise using the expressions by talking about different places, and where it is convenient to stay.

1 Role play 1 is for two speakers.

A works at the Khania Tourist Office.

B works for Golfreisen tour operators in Stuttgart, Germany.

A looks at this page. B turns to page 81.

SPEAKER A

Role play 1

You get a phone call from B, who has received information about Khania and the golf course, but would like more. Answer B's questions using the information below.

Hotel and number of stars	Place	Type	Distance from golf course
Khania Palace****	Ayios Marina	very modern, air-conditioning	1 km E
Athena****	Khania port	traditional, one of oldest hotels in Khania	5 km E
Apollo***	Kolimvari	15 years old but clean and efficient	25 km W
Helena**	Ayios Marina	old-style, friendly, family-run	opposite golf course entrance

KEY VOCABULARY

Hotels

Match the words on the left with the words on the right to make expressions relating to hotels, allowing you to do the things listed in a–f below.

1 air   pool
2 full   desk
3 reception   board
4 room   facilities
5 sports   service
6 swimming   conditioning

a) get food and drink delivered to your room
b) sunbathe
c) stay cool
d) get fit
e) check in and out
f) eat all meals at the hotel

2 Role play 2 is a series of telephone conversations for two speakers.

A takes the parts of three different people who phone Golfreisen tour operators to ask about hotels near the Khania golf course.

B works for Golfreisen.

A looks at this page. B turns to page 81.

SPEAKER A

Role play 2

Note: in one case, you may not be able to get what you are looking for.

1 You are looking for a hotel:
   • quite near the golf course
   • without a pool (you don't like the sound of people shouting in the pool)
   • with or without air-conditioning
   • with or without full board: it doesn't matter

2 You are looking for a hotel:
   • up to 30 km from the golf course
   • with a pool
   • without air-conditioning (it makes you feel ill)
   • without a restaurant (you don't like the smell of food cooking all day)

3 You are looking for a hotel:
   • not too far from the golf course
   • with a pool
   • with air-conditioning
   • with full board (you don't want to leave the hotel except to go to the course)

In the news

KEY VOCABULARY

Protest

Complete the definitions using the correct grammatical forms of the words in **bold**. (Sometimes the related form is the same as the form in bold.)

1 People who **oppose** something are _____ of it and form the _____ to it.

2 **Extremism** is where a few people, called _____s, have much stronger views than most people's. These opinions are _____.

3 People who say in public that they are against something **protest** against it and are _____s. They take part in _____s.

4 Protests may take the form of **demonstrations**: people marching down the street, carrying banners, shouting slogans, etc. These people are _____ and what they do is to _____.

5 If people **confront** each other verbally or physically, there is a _____.

6 Similarly, if people **clash**, there is a _____, a disagreement between them that may be verbal or physical.

7 When demonstrations become violent, people taking part in them may **riot** by behaving violently, smashing shop windows, burning parked cars, etc. When this happens there are _____s and the participants are _____s.

8 If people steal things from shops and homes during riots, there is **looting** and the people doing this are _____s.

A Listening

1 🎧 You will hear five items of business news from a business programme on the radio. Match each item (1–5) with one of the headings (a–h).

1 _____
2 _____
3 _____
4 _____
5 _____

a) currencies
b) environmental protest
c) house prices
d) industrial relations
e) inflation
f) share indexes
g) mergers and acquisitions
h) unemployment

2 🎧 ◄UNIT 3► Listen to the recording of a news programme about Hermosa and choose the correct alternatives to answer the questions.

1 When the demonstrations started they were _____.
a) peaceful   b) noisy   c) violent

2 Which of these events was *not* mentioned as having been stolen by looters?
a) cars   b) electrical goods   c) food

3 The police may have over-reacted towards the demonstrators. This means they may have been too _____.
a) peaceful   b) slow to act   c) violent

4 Susie Tan says that the demonstrators _____.
a) were right to act as they did
b) should remember the importance of investment in the region
c) should take more extreme action

5 The reporter says that, at the time she is speaking, the rioting _____.
a) is continuing
b) has stopped and the atmosphere is good
c) has stopped but the atmosphere is bad

6 The reporter says that environmental protest around the world is becoming

_____.

a) more organised   b) more violent   c) more effective

3 🎧 Listen to the interview with Rebecca Chu and mark the statements T (true), F (false) or DK (we don't know).

1 Demonstrations around Hermosa in the past year have been co-ordinated by Green Action.	T	F	DK
2 The demonstration last night in Puerto Escondido was organised by Green Action.	T	F	DK
3 Demonstrators have occupied the site of the proposed refinery.	T	F	DK
4 They say they will stay on the site for another year, and then leave.	T	F	DK
5 The Hermosan Ministry of Industry is willing to consider other sites.	T	F	DK
6 The site at Puerto Escondido is the only suitable site on the island, according to the Ministry of Industry.	T	F	DK
7 The Ministry of Industry says the refinery is necessary for living standards to go on rising.	T	F	DK
8 The west coast has already been fully developed for tourism.	T	F	DK
9 Big industrial projects are considered important by developing countries.	T	F	DK
10 Big industrial projects are economically justified.	T	F	DK

Speaking

Making your point

Match the two parts of these sentences containing expressions for making your point in a discussion.

1 **I believe that** building the refinery	A the local economy to develop.
2 **Personally, I think that** the refinery will help	B underestimated local opposition to the plan.
3 **As I see it**, we must choose between tourism and heavy industry:	C influence than they realise.
4 **It looks to me as if** the ministry has	D we can't have both.
5 **In my opinion**, hotel owners here have more	E than environmental organisations, but this is changing.
6 **It's clear to me** that the government have not thought	F tanker accident and the beaches will be polluted.
7 **Obviously**, governments have more power	G about the long-term effects of the plan.
8 **Of course**, one day there will be a	H here will be a disaster.

1 Imagine you are one of the people below. Use the expressions in **bold** above to put their point of view.

A **Industry minister.** Refinery necessary for economic development – environmental protesters are enemies of development and higher living standards – government will not give way to "environmental terrorism"

Oil industry spokesperson. No other site on the island has deep enough water for large tankers – danger to the environment overestimated – strict controls on tankers' movements, loading and unloading – refinery will have highest environmental standards

Mayor of Puerto Escondido. Refinery will help open up west of island – tourism should not be the only industry – Hermosan economy currently too centred on east coast – will increase number of jobs in the area – increased prosperity

B **Resident of Puerto Escondido.** Strange place to put a refinery – very near beaches – tourism very important economically, more important than heavy industry – support peaceful protest and "sympathise" with protesters who have occupied site of refinery but not violent demonstrators

Head of environmental group Green Action. Environmental controls always break down sooner or later – growth not the goal but quality of life – support peaceful protest and "understand" those who have occupied the site of refinery – don't support violent protest

Member of extremist environmental group. People accuse us of being extremist – government and industry are the extremists, damaging the environment – soon whole of Hermosa covered in concrete and industry – all actions to stop this justified – must go back to simpler lifestyle of farming and fishing

KEY EXPRESSIONS

Developing your point

Match the two parts of these extracts containing expressions for developing your point in a discussion.

1 The rioting has **not only** caused a lot of damage to buildings,

2 Using the police damages the popularity of the government.

3 **On (the) one hand**, the government wants the money from tourism,

4 The refinery will help open up the west coast.

5 This is the only place where the water is deep enough.

6 We can't go back to living on fishing and farming: it means going back to poverty and ignorance. And

7 Occupying the site prevents it from being developed.

8 I sympathise with people who occupy the site.

A and **on the other hand**, they talk about the benefits of this refinery. It's not logical.

B **but also** it has damaged the image of the protesters.

C **And another thing**: using the police encourages people to use violent methods of protest.

D **apart from that**, an economy based on fishing and farming is just not a realistic possibility in a global economy.

E **However**, I don't agree with damaging property.

F **Besides that**, the site on land is perfect for a development like this.

G **In addition**, it will help the economy develop as a whole.

H **What's more**, it provides good pictures on television.

2 Keep the same role and use the expressions in *Developing your point* to develop the points you made in Exercise 1 above.

3 This role play is for two speakers.

A is one of the people in Group A in Exercise 1.

B is one of the people in Group B.

Construct a conversation between these two people.

KEY VOCABULARY

Discussion and argument

Read this, paying attention to the words and expressions in **bold**.

The industry minister discussed the refinery with the head of an environmental group. Each person **made his point**. There were **differences of opinion**. In fact, they could not **agree** about anything. The **discussion** turned into an **argument**: the minister and the environmentalist become angry and **lost their tempers**. The **argument** ended with them continuing to disagree. There was no **consensus**, a set of opinions that they could both agree with.

4 Now use the expressions above, in the correct grammatical forms, to talk about the discussion (or argument!) you had in Exercise 3 above.

C Reading and writing

Proposals

Complete the definitions using the expressions in the box.

> carried out   consulted   dropped   imposed
> modified   rejected   thrown out

1 If people who are going to be affected by a proposal are asked what they think of it, they are _____ about it.

2 If a proposal is changed, it is _____.

3 If a proposal is put into action, it is _____.

4 If a proposal is put into action against the wishes of the people it affects, it is _____.

5 If a proposal is abandoned, it is _____.

6 If a proposal is not accepted, it is _____ or _____.

1 Read this memo by an environmental activist to the head of her environmental organisation, Green Action. Choose the best title for each numbered paragraph from a–g on page 57.

MEMO

GREEN ACTION

To: Charles Chang, Director, Green Action
From: Mary Goncalves, West Coast Action Co-ordinator

1 Following the decision of the authorities to abandon plans for the refinery near Puerto Escondido, we are right to celebrate. Very serious damage to the environment has been avoided. Most local people are very happy that the refinery is not going ahead. Two years of protests have finally paid off. The government realised that they could no longer defend their position. Thanks in part to our research work on the future oil needs of Hermosa, they were persuaded that a new refinery was not needed, and Hermosa's oil needs can be satisfied using existing facilities. We showed that Green Action could play a full part in influencing decisions about the development of the Hermosan economy.

2 The policy of occupying the site of the proposed refinery was also very important. It makes very good pictures on television and catches the attention of ordinary people.

3 However, we cannot stop here. The government has decided to make tourism the priority here, and that, they say, means improving the infrastructure. Plans include the expansion of the airport at Puerto Escondido so that it can handle the biggest aircraft, and the building of a six-lane motorway along the coast from Puerto Escondido to the south. I spoke to someone from the Department of Tourism who said that these developments are essential if, in his words, "we want to make the west coast a world-class tourist centre".

4 So far, tourist development has not been too bad. Tourist hotels are designed to go well with the landscape. The continuous concrete development of some Mediterranean coasts has been avoided, so far at least. We must do everything we can to make sure that development continues in this way. However, we must not be seen as being against tourism, as a lot of people make their living from it here.

5 We must remain in touch with Hector Fung of the West Coast Preservation Society. Together we will successfully oppose these two new projects. We have learnt a lot about successful protest in the last two years and we will get these projects thrown out.

Paragraph 1 _____

Paragraph 2 _____

Paragraph 3 _____

Paragraph 4 _____

Paragraph 5 _____

a) Tourist development in the Mediterranean
b) The importance of taking forms of action that interest ordinary people
c) Site occupation methods
d) Government plans for the west coast
e) Future co-ordination with other organisations
f) Ensuring that Green Action is not seen as being against tourism
g) Evaluation of our action so far

2 Using information from the memo in Exercise 1, complete each sentence with a phrase from the list below.

1 Charles Chang thinks that the government changed its mind about the refinery

_____.

2 The protest action against the refinery was successful but _____.

3 Green Action should protest against the new developments but _____.

4 Green Action has learnt a lot in the last few years and _____.

a) thanks entirely to Green Action's efforts
b) should now look at new methods of protest
c) partly because of Green Action's protests
d) more action is needed to prevent further new developments
e) it can successfully protest against the new developments
f) because of economic problems
g) avoid making people think that it is against tourism

3 You own and run a hotel on Hermosa's west coast. Write a report of about 150 words to Mary Goncalves at Green Action about the motorway and airport expansion proposals, expressing the following opinions:

• Say that you support the new motorway and airport expansion.
• Give your reasons for supporting the motorway project: existing road very dangerous – tourists spend a lot of time stuck in traffic – will bring construction jobs to the west coast – will allow further development of tourism on the west coast.
• Give your reasons for supporting airport expansion: airport currently very crowded and congested – tourists waste a lot of time in the airport – present airport gives a very bad impression of Hermosa when people arrive for the first time – bigger planes cannot use it.
• Close appropriately, saying that you hope Green Action will reconsider its position.

Good times and bad

slumps and recessions

job cuts and redundancies

motivation and morale

career development

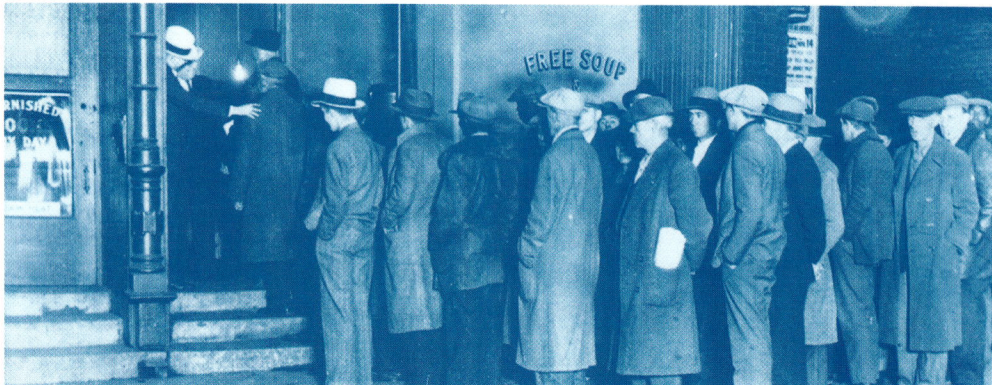

KEY VOCABULARY

Booms and recessions

Complete the commentary using the words in the box. One of the words is used twice.

| boom | demand | downturns | recession | slump |

The amount of goods and services that are bought in an economy at a particular time is the level of (1) _____. For example, in Europe and the US during the 1920s, there was a (2) _____ with rising (3) _____ for goods or services and people felt good about the economy.

A (4) _____ is a period when there is negative growth, when an industry or the economy as whole is getting smaller. If the recession is very bad, there is a (5) _____. Following the Wall Street Crash of 1929, there was a long depression with falling production, and millions of people out of work.

There have been other recessions when there have been relatively small _____ (6) in the economy, but nothing as bad as the Great Depression of the 1930s.

A Listening

1 🎧 Listen to the extracts about different industries. Which industry is mentioned in each extract? Is demand for its products or services growing (+) or declining (–)? The first one has been done as an example.

Industry	+/–
1 *cars*	+
2	
3	
4	
5	

KEY VOCABULARY

Redundancy

Choose the correct alternative to complete the following definitions.

1 When there are too many factories producing particular products, there is

_____.

 a) added capacity   b) overcapacity   c) plus capacity

2 When a company stops employing people it makes them _____.
 a) useless   b) redundant   c) unnecessary

3 The normal expression for the situation where people are forced to leave their

 jobs is _____.
 a) compulsory redundancy
 b) forced redundancy
 c) obligatory redundancy

4 The normal expression for the situation where people are given the choice to

 leave their job is _____.
 a) chosen redundancy   b) voluntary redundancy   c) wished redundancy

5 When a company stops employing people, either temporarily or permanently,

 it lays them _____.
 a) down   b) out   c) off

6 When a company stops employing people permanently, it may talk about

 letting them _____.
 a) depart   b) leave   c) go

7 When a company reduces the number of employees over time by not replacing

 those who leave, it refers to _____.
 a) natural disappearance   b) natural departures   c) natural wastage

2 🎧 ◄UNIT 4► Listen to this radio programme about Random Semiconductors, and mark the statements true or false.

1 Random is going to close its site outside Dublin completely.	T	F
2 The news of changes at Random came completely unexpectedly.	T	F
3 More than half of Random's production of processors is used in personal computers.	T	F
4 Robyn Ashley says that people are buying fewer PCs because they have less money to spend.	T	F
5 Robyn Ashley says that people only want PCs for internet access and nothing else.	T	F
6 She thinks that Random may one day increase production again in Ireland.	T	F
7 Random say that they will attempt to reduce the number of employees through voluntary redundancies and natural wastage.	T	F
8 All former Random employees will all be able to find work extremely easily again in the Dublin area.	T	F
9 Robyn mentions suppliers of delivery services among those suppliers likely to be affected.	T	F
10 The housing market near Random will be affected.	T	F

Reading and writing

KEY VOCABULARY

Human resources

1 Combine the words on the left with the words on the right to form compounds that match definitions a–f below.

1	relocation	services
2	redundancy	resources
3	payroll	costs
4	outplacement	cuts
5	salary	package
6	human	bill

a) the department in a company that is sometimes called "personnel"
b) all the benefits that a company offers when someone is asked to leave their job
c) expenses relating to moving from one place to another when changing jobs
d) the help that specialised agencies give to people who have to leave a job so that they can find a new one
e) reducing the number of people working for a company, and the cost of paying them
f) the total amount paid to a company's employees in a particular period

1 Choose the correct alternative from 1–10 on page 61 to fill each gap in the letter.

RANDOM SEMICONDUCTORS
Human Resources Department
Liffey Business Park, Dublin, Ireland

June 6

Dear Colleague,

As you are probably aware, the global demand for processors has declined dramatically in the last year. Like all other manufacturers in the industry, we have been badly hit by this slump. With our (1) _____ at headquarters, we have discussed the various possibilities open to us. After examining the situation extremely carefully, we have unfortunately come to the (2) _____ that if Random is to remain in business in Ireland, (3) _____ are the only option available to us.

We had been hoping to reduce the payroll by (4) _____ wastage, but this process would take too long. We need to make payroll cuts immediately in order to reduce our total (5) _____ bill.

I am therefore writing to you to suggest a voluntary redundancy (6) _____.
We will pay two months' salary for each year you have worked here. We will also put you in contact with an outplacement (7) _____ in Dublin to assist you in finding a new position. We will pay for (8) _____ should you decide to take up a new position using their services.

We appreciate the (9) _____ that Random's employees have shown in the past and how much they have contributed to our success. This development comes as a bitter (10) _____ to us all. However, if you wish to discuss the terms of voluntary redundancy, please contact me.

Yours sincerely,

Mary O'Reilly

Mary O'Reilly
Director, Human Resources

1 a) comrades	b) colleagues	c) compatriots	d) connoisseurs
2 a) conclusion	b) ending	c) finding	d) point
3 a) departures	b) leavings	c) redundancies	d) redundancy
4 a) everyday	b) ordinary	c) organic	d) natural
5 a) employment	b) employee	c) job	d) salary
6 a) pack	b) package	c) packet	d) parcel
7 a) consult	b) consultation	c) consultancy	d) construction
8 a) relocation	b) repositioning	c) resiting	d) resitting
9 a) committal	b) commitment	c) engagement	d) implication
10 a) disappointment	b) disenchantment	c) distress	d) distaste

2 Read the letter again and mark the following statements true or false.

1 The writer of the letter thinks that employees do not know about
  Random's problems.   T   F
2 The fall in demand for processors has been small.   T   F
3 Making people redundant is just one of the options that Random has
  considered.   T   F
4 Making people redundant is the only cost-cutting measure that will work. T   F
5 Natural wastage is the immediate solution to the problem of
  reducing costs.   T   F
6 Random is not forcing people to take the redundancy package.   T   F
7 If an employee takes the redundancy package and has worked for
  three years at Random, he or she will get six months' salary.   T   F
8 Employees will pay for the outplacement service if they find a new
  job by using it.   T   F
9 Random is grateful to its employees for the work they have done.   T   F
10 The writer of the letter wants everyone who reads it to reply.   T   F

3 You are a production line employee at Random and you receive the letter in
Exercise 1. Write a reply, including these points:

- You think Random is making a mistake in making experienced people redundant.
- You think the voluntary redundancy package is a form of bribe.
- You think Random should keep as many employees as possible and wait for an
  improvement in business.
- Say politely that you do not want to accept the package.
- Close appropriately.

4 You are a manager at Random and you receive the letter in Exercise 1. Write a
reply, including these points:

- You would like to accept the redundancy package.
- Ask for an appointment with someone in the human resources department to
  discuss the package.
- Ask about the services that the outplacement consultancy can offer.
- Ask how much is typically paid in relocation costs.
- Say you share Mary O'Reilly's disappointment at the need for redundancies.
- Close appropriately.

C Speaking

Motivation and morale

Complete the definitions using the words in the box.

> committed   incentive   morale   motivation   perform

If you want to work hard because you find the work interesting, you are *motivated*. The corresponding noun is (1) _____. A related word is *commitment*. If people feel (2) _____ to their job and their organisation, they want to work hard so that the organisation is successful.

The way that people work and how well they work is their *performance*.

People are sometimes paid according to how they (3) _____: how well they work, how much they produce, etc.

If people have a particular reason to work hard, they have an (4) _____ to work hard.

How people in general are feeling in an organisation is their (5) _____. This can be good or bad.

1 Role play 1 is for two speakers.

A is Nicole Pelissier. B is Leslie MacFadden.

You both joined Random at the same time, three years ago.

You now know each other quite well. (You play golf together.)

You are having lunch in the Random canteen. You have both been offered voluntary redundancy packages.

Have a conversation based on the role play notes.

A looks at this page. B turns to page 82.

SPEAKER A

Role play 1

You don't want to accept the redundancy package.
- You moved to Dublin with your Irish partner, who doesn't want to leave Ireland again.
- You like it in Ireland (even the climate!).
- You feel motivated in your job (materials buyer/planner), despite the company's problems.
- You like the lifestyle: golf, lack of stress, etc.
- You don't want to move or look for another job.
- You think the company is short-sighted (not thinking about the future enough) in making experienced people redundant.
- You think the company will regret having lost these people when business improves.
- Morale in your department is very bad.

KEY QUESTIONS AND ANSWERS

Career development

Someone is being interviewed about their career so far and their future plans.
Match the questions on the left with the answers on the right.

1 How do you feel about your time in the company?

2 What do you think were your most important achievements?

3 What was your biggest disappointment?

4 How do you see your career developing in the immediate future?

5 Where do you see yourself ten years from now?

A I think my main achievement was that in addition to the technical training, we set up a programme of high-quality management training.

B I was disappointed by the fact that, recently, there were big cuts in the training budget.

C Right now, I'd like a complete change.

D Perhaps I will have found something much less stressful.

E On the one hand my time there was very stimulating. But on the other it was demoralising.

2 Role play 2 is for two speakers.

A is the outplacement consultant used by Random Semiconductors to help people who have chosen voluntary redundancy to find jobs.

B is Leslie MacFadden.

Discuss B's time at Random and plans for the future.

A looks at this page. B turns to page 82.

SPEAKER A

Role play 2

Below is the latest version of Leslie MacFadden's CV.
Using questions similar to those above, find out:
- more about Leslie MacFadden's time at Random, under the three headings *recruitment, development of management training, budgets*
- his plans for the immediate future
- what he would like to be doing ten years from now

Leslie MacFadden

2001–present **Head of training, Random Semiconductors**
- recruited and managed team of ten in-house technical trainers
- developed management training with support of senior managers
- responsible for budgets and selection of outside training providers

1993–2001 **Trainer, Bell PCs, Dublin**
One of team of seven trainers at Bell Assembly plant. Planning and scheduling of wide range of management and technical courses.

1987–93 **Physics teacher, Galway High School**
Gave physics lessons at all levels of school, including leaving certificate level.

1986–87 **University College, Galway**
Trained to teach physics in secondary schools.

1983–86 **Midwestern University, Chicago**
Degree in physics.

1981–83 **Lakeside High School, Chicago**

Good interpersonal skills with all levels of employees and management

Interests: baseball, Irish football (amateur player), golf, folk guitar

2+2=5?

voicemail messages

plans and consequences

comparing and contrasting

UNIT 11

Takeovers and mergers

Takeovers and mergers

Complete the commentary using the expressions in the box.

acquisitions	friendly	merger	predator
prey	takeover	target company	

When one company buys another, it takes it over. If the shareholders of the

(1) _____ (the company being taken over) do not

want this, the (2) _____ is hostile. If they do, it is (3) _____.

   A company that often takes over or acquires others is said to be *acquisitive*.

The companies it buys are (4) _____. It may be referred to, especially

by journalists, as a (5) _____, and the companies it buys, or would like

to buy, as its (6) _____.

   If two companies combine as equals, they join together in a (7) _____.

A   Listening

1 🎧 ◀UNIT 5▶   It's just been announced that Francisco Guerrero's company
Flyaway Airlines has taken over a Swiss airline called White Cross Airways.

Guerrero's secretary has been out of the office and she returns to find five
messages on her boss's voicemail. For each message, complete the notes that she
makes under these headings. If a piece of information is not given, write NG.

	Name of caller	Caller's organisation	Caller's number	Purpose of call
1				
2				
3				
4				
5				

2 🎧   Francisco Guerrero, founder of Flyaway Airlines, is interviewed about his
airline's takeover of White Cross Airways. Listen to the interview once, and write
down the figures that he mentions.

1 White Cross Airways' sales last year: _____ Swiss francs

2 White Cross Airways' loss last year: _____ Swiss francs

3 number of routes currently run by White Cross Airways: _____

4 people living within two hours of Geneva: _____

5 loss-making European airlines that are potential takeover targets:

_____

6 passengers using Geneva airport last year: _____

7 passengers using Heathrow airport last year: _____

8 planes taking off and landing at Geneva last year: _____

9 planes taking off and landing at Heathrow last year: _____

3 Listen to the interview again and choose the correct alternatives to answer the questions.

1 When Guerrero says that he hopes to turn the situation round, he means that

he hopes to _____.
a) sell White Cross   b) make it profitable   c) close it down

2 On Flyaway's flights, coffee is _____.
a) free   b) unavailable   c) paid for by passengers

3 Potential customers are ones who _____.
a) already use the airline   b) may use it   c) will definitely use it

4 Geneva airport _____.
a) is being used as much as it can be
b) could be used much more
c) is inconvenient

5 A hub is an airport _____.
a) near a city where people want to go for business
b) near another airport
c) where people can easily change planes to fly on to somewhere else

6 Guerrero thinks that, for his company, a direct flight from London to Sofia

would _____.
a) definitely be profitable
b) perhaps be unprofitable
c) be neither profitable nor unprofitable

7 In talking about room for expansion at Geneva, Guerrero talks about Heathrow

because _____.
a) he wants his airline to be able to use Heathrow
b) he wants to give an idea of the size and potential for Geneva by comparing
   it with Heathrow
c) there are flights from Heathrow to Geneva

8 When the interviewer asks if Guerrero has plans for other acquisitions, he also

uses the word "prey". In this context, prey means _____.
a) acquisitions   b) passengers   c) aircraft

9 Guerrero would like to get into the transatlantic market. He would like to offer

flights from Europe to _____.
a) Africa   b) the Middle East   c) North America

10 How have the national airlines reacted to the takeover?
a) They think it's a good thing.
b) They think it's unfair.
c) They don't mind.

B Reading and writing

1 A few months after Flyaway's takeover of White Cross, Flyaway merged with another airline, Atlantic Air. Read this article about the merger and complete the table below. If something is not mentioned in the article, write NM.

SURPRISE MERGER BETWEEN FLYAWAY AND ATLANTIC AIR

In a surprise move, only a few months after its acquisition of Geneva-based White Cross Airways, Flyaway Airlines today announced that it is merging with Atlantic Air. Flyaway chairman Francisco Guerrero and the head of Atlantic, Barbara Walters, appeared together at a press conference in London to announce the deal. "This is a dream tie-up," said Mr Guerrero. "We have always wanted to get into the transatlantic market, and this is an ideal way of doing it." Ms Walters was equally enthusiastic: "Combining our operations will allow the new company to build its operations in Europe. Passengers will be able to transfer from Flyaway's European flights onto our flights to North America. We also plan to start direct flights from European cities to the United States when regulations permit this."

The new airline, to be called Flyaway Atlantic, brings together two very different companies. Atlantic has been in business for nearly 20 years and is the fourth-biggest carrier on Atlantic routes. Based at London's second airport, Gatwick, it's what could be called a "traditional" airline: it sells tickets mainly through travel agents and has only recently begun to take bookings over the internet. It has full cabin service on all its flights, with a choice of meals in all classes. Airline staff wear traditional dark blue uniforms.

Flyaway was founded only seven years ago by Mr Guerrero, who has become known for his outspoken views on airline competition. The company has grown rapidly and last year acquired Geneva-based White Cross Airways. Flyaway currently operates 23 routes out of Croydon airport, near London, as well as ten routes between other European cities. It is famous for its basic but reliable and punctual services. There are no meals on board, and if you want coffee, you pay 50 pence for the privilege. Flyaway's staff are famous for their bright yellow jackets.

It will be interesting to see how these two very different organisations get on when they try to combine their operations. Atlantic is reported to have average costs in relation to airlines in general, but they are certainly higher than Flyaway's. Mr Guerrero's office is in a temporary building next to the runways at Croydon airport. Flyaway has no prestigious offices in London, and no sales offices where passengers can book in person, as all flights are booked by phone and over the internet. Atlantic, on the other hand, has its headquarters and a sales office in central London, and sales offices in the downtown areas of five North American cities.

	Flyaway	Atlantic Air
1 Location of headquarters		
2 Where airline flies from		
3 Age of airline		
4 Costs in relation to other airlines		
5 Total number of routes		
6 How tickets are sold		
7 Food and drinks on board		
8 Punctuality and reliability		

2 Complete each gap in this report with one of the sentences a–h below.

■ WHEN CULTURES CLASH ──────────────────────

When the London Financial Press (FP) merged five years ago with Le Magazine des Affaires (MdA) in Paris, the head of the Financial Press was appointed to run the two newspapers. She went to MdA's offices in Paris to explain the deal to employees there. She spoke in English, and there was no interpreter. (1) _____. But people in the Paris office were angry that she spoke to them in English. Somehow the co-operation between the two papers never materialised, and they remained, in effect, separate organisations. Today, FPMdA's share price is only 10 per cent higher than it was at the time of the merger, while the stockmarket as a whole has increased by 70 per cent.

It's not only a question of language. When a German car company merges with an American one, there are two very different management styles, and two very different ways of organising companies from a legal point of view. German companies have two boards of directors: one for the day-to-day running of the company, and another "supervisory" board above it. (2) _____.

And when the language is the same, or almost, there can still be problems. A British oil company takes over an American one. A lot of American executives are fired. (3) _____.

These are all examples of mergers and takeovers between companies in the same industry. What happens when they take place between companies in different industries? (4) _____. The average age of the managers in the internet company is 33 and they wear T-shirts; in the media group, it's 45, and they wear suits. (5) _____. They may end up being irritated by the "inexperience" and "immaturity" of their younger colleagues. ■

a) Americans aren't used to this arrangement and may find it strange.

b) An American internet company takes over a "traditional" US media group that produces films, and owns television companies and newspapers.

c) She had no bad news to announce: in fact she announced plans for expansion and investment by the two newspapers.

d) Some of them could speak German, but they had learnt it a long time ago.

e) Studies have never been done on mergers between companies in different industries.

f) Suits are smarter than T-shirts, and give a better impression, especially in the United States.

g) The older managers in the media group start by hoping that the internet people are going to find new ways of distributing their films, TV programmes and newspaper articles.

h) The ones who stay don't like the atmosphere, feel less motivated and start looking for new jobs in other companies.

3 You have just left a company that merged with another company six months ago. You didn't like the way things were changing.

Write an e-mail to a friend. Start by explaining what has happened and then describe how you felt that the managers from the other company:

- dressed too casually: the men didn't wear a tie and the women wore jeans
- were too familiar when they talked to colleagues and didn't show enough respect
- didn't respect their bosses enough
- always turned up five or ten minutes late for meetings
- always interrupted other people in meetings
- didn't work enough and went home too early

Close appropriately and say what sort of company you are hoping to work for next.

C Speaking

Plans and consequences

Complete the summary using the correct forms of the words in brackets (or of words related to them). Each dash represents one letter.

When you decide to do something and take (1) _ _ _ _ _ o n *(act)*, you never quite know what it's going to lead to. When a plan is (2) _ _ _ _ _ _ _ d _ _ _ *(carry out)*, it may or may not be (3) _ _ _ _ _ _ _ _ v e *(effect)*. It may have the effects that were (4) _ _ _ _ n _ _ *(plan)*, but it will probably also have other, additional (5) _ _ _ _ _ _ _ _ _ c e s *(consequent)*, some of which you may not even have (6) _ _ _ _ _ _ _ n *(foresee)*.

This is true of mergers. Studies show that the (7) _ _ _ _ _ _ d _ _ *(intention)* benefits are often not realised in practice.

1 Use these notes to talk about some mergers and takeovers. Talk about what was *planned* (the intention) and what *actually happened* (the outcome).

For example:

> AOL bought Netscape's browser for $4 billion so that its members could access the internet using Netscape rather than Microsoft Internet Explorer. But what actually happened is that AOL members are still using Explorer, and it's hard to see what benefits AOL has gained from buying Netscape.

Companies involved	Industry	Intention	Outcome
AOL/Netscape	internet access providers	allow AOL customers to use Netscape as internet browser to access the internet, instead of Microsoft Explorer	AOL customers still using Explorer. Hard to see benefits for AOL
Pricewaterhouse/ Coopers & Lybrand	accountancy/ consulting	build global accounting and consultancy firm, reduce costs	higher costs than expected in combining operations
Daimler/Chrysler	cars/trucks	cut costs; build global presence	many good US executives have left; felt company was being run from Germany, not as an equal partnership
Pharmacia/ Upjohn	pharmaceuticals	combine research resources, reduce costs, produce new drugs	cultural problems between Swedes and Americans
Disney/Infoseek	internet content and access	Disney paid $3 billion for Infoseek, which allows users to search for information on internet	not clear how Infoseek helps Disney

2 This role play is for two speakers.

Two companies, Uptight Inc and Laidback Co, are going to merge.

A is an expert on Uptight and B is an expert on Laidback.

A and B exchange information about the two companies.

A looks at this page. B turns to page 83.

SPEAKER A

Ask B questions and complete the information about Laidback Co.

	Uptight Inc	Laidback Co
Dress	Fairly formal. Men wear dark suits. Women always dresses or skirts, never trousers.	
Working hours	Everybody, even managers, clocks in and out, putting a card in a computerised time clock. Flexible working time within certain limits so as to do an average of 40 hours per week.	
Decision-making	Junior members of staff not usually consulted. Decisions imposed from above.	
Communication	E-mail only just introduced. Very few people use it. Fax still widely used.	
Meetings	Internal meetings usually planned days or weeks in advance. Meeting rooms booked, with sandwiches and refreshments provided.	
Entertaining	Clients are often taken to the best restaurant in town. Managers rarely invite clients (or each other) to their own homes.	

KEY EXPRESSIONS

Comparing and contrasting

Now use these expressions to compare and contrast Uptight and Laidback in a short presentation.

But …
Whereas …
In contrast …
By comparison …
On the other hand …

For example:
Men at Uptight tend to wear a suit and tie, whereas at Laidback, dress is more casual.

Doing deals

social language

negotiation

reaching and confirming
agreement

KEY EXPRESSIONS

What to say after you say hello

Match the two parts of these exchanges.

1 Here's my card.
2 Can I give you a lift somewhere?
3 How about lunch one day next
   week?
4 Would you like to see our
   catalogue?
5 I'll put you in touch with a
   colleague who deals with this.
6 Excuse me. Are you Agneta
   Dahlquist? Ingvar Jonsson told
   me you would be here.
7 You'll never guess who I
   bumped into on the plane.

A Shall we say Luigi's on Friday at one?
B And here's mine.
C It's OK thanks. It's a long way. I'll
   get a cab.
D Yes, I'd like to meet them.
E You must be Ewa Kowalska.
   Pleased to meet you.
F No, who?
G Mmm … it looks very interesting.

A Listening

1 🎧 ◄UNIT 6► Ewa Kowalska, Sales Director of Meblopol, the Polish furniture
   manufacturer, is on a plane to Stockholm. Listen to the recording once and say
   which of these names you hear in the recording, and which you do not hear.

   ____ *Financial Press*   ____ *Financial Journal*

   ____ Ingemar Johansson   ____ Ingvar Jonsson

   ____ Anna Nowak   ____ Ewa Kowalska

   ____ Agneta Dahlquist   ____ Agneta Dahlgren

   ____ Sollentuna   ____ Solna

   ____ Meblex   ____ Meblopol

2 Listen to the recording again and mark the statements true or false.

   1 Ingvar Jonsson doesn't think there's much news in the *Financial
      Press* today.   T   F
   2 He likes publicity for himself.   T   F
   3 Milieu has just opened its third store in Poland.   T   F
   4 Jonsson spends all of his time at head office and rarely travels.   T   F
   5 Ewa Kowalska is Sales Director of her company.   T   F
   6 She's going to Stockholm for a short holiday.   T   F
   7 Her company made a profit of 30 million euros last year.   T   F
   8 She started her business in 1993.   T   F
   9 Milieu wants to sell more office furniture.   T   F
   10 Jonsson suggests that she meets Milieu's Financial Director.   T   F
   11 He suggests that Ewa Kowalska should come to Milieu's offices.   T   F
   12 Milieu's offices are in the centre of Stockholm.   T   F

3 Choose the most tactful, polite or suitable response in a business context to 1–6 below.

1 You found us OK then.
   a) It was a nightmare.
   b) No problem at all.
   c) It took me hours to get out here.

2 Can I introduce you to Agneta Dahlquist?
   a) How very wonderful to meet you.
   b) Charmed, I'm sure.
   c) Good to meet you.

3 And now, if you'll excuse me, I'll leave you to it.
   a) Yes, you go and get on with what you have to do.
   b) No problem. Nice seeing you again.
   c) Don't leave us whatever you do.

4 Thanks for asking me to come out here.
   a) It's a pleasure.   b) I was in a good mood.   c) Please.

5 I hope we can do business together.
   a) Well, it depends.   b) I must check your background.   c) Yes, I hope so.

6 Can I get you something? Tea, coffee, juice, mineral water?
   a) Give me juice.
   b) Some tea would be nice.
   c) You don't have any beer, I suppose?

4 🎧 Ewa Kowalska arrives at Milieu's head office for her meeting with Agneta Dahlquist.

Are the expressions in 1–8 exactly the ones you hear on the recording? Tick the ones that are exactly the same, and write out the ones that are different.

1 You found us OK then.

   _____

2 Can I introduce you to Agneta Dahlquist?

   _____

3 And now, if you'll excuse me, I'll leave you two to get on with it.

   _____

4 Thanks for asking me to come out here.

   _____

5 I hope we can do business together.

   _____

6 Shall we go up to my office?

   _____

7 Can I get you something? Tea, coffee, juice, mineral water?

   _____

8 Let's get down to business, shall we?

   _____

Speaking and writing

Negotiation

A buyer and a supplier are negotiating an agreement. Match the expressions on the left (used by the buyer) with the responses on the right (used by the supplier).

1 **So, we're going to talk about** price and delivery for office desks, right?

2 **If we** commit to ordering 7,000 units a year, would you be willing to look at a lower price?

3 **I think** the initial agreement **should** be for two years.

4 **So we're agreed on** specifications, then.

5 Let's move on to delivery dates. **It's essential** for us to have the first delivery in three months.

6 **We could accept** first deliveries in four months, no more.

7 **Right, let's summarise** what we've agreed.

A **If you agree to** three years, **I could** bring down the price even further.

B **I think today we should concentrate on** exact specifications and price, and come back to payment conditions another time.

C Yes, **I think we've covered** specs.

D **To be frank** five months is more realistic: we need time to prepare for production.

E **Shall we split the difference** and say four and a half?

F Yes, a quick summary **would be useful**.

G **How about** ordering 9,000 units? Then we could give you an even bigger price reduction.

Now match the exchanges above with these stages in the negotiation. B is the buyer and S is the supplier.

a) B **makes a concession** on delivery and S makes another **concession**.

b) B makes a **proposal** about the number they are prepared to buy, asking for a price reduction, and S makes a **counter-proposal**.

c) B makes an **offer** on the initial period to be covered by the agreement, and S makes a **counter-offer**.

d) B says that they have **reached agreement** on specifications, and S confirms this.

e) B **states their position** firmly on delivery and S **reacts** firmly.

f) B suggests that they **summarise** what has been agreed and S confirms that this would be useful.

g) The two sides agree on the **subjects to be covered** in the negotiation.

1 This role play is for two speakers.

A is a buyer for Milieu, the large furniture chain with 60 large stores worldwide.

B represents a furniture manufacturer who wants an agreement to supply office desks to Milieu over a period. These desks will be specially designed for Milieu.

A looks at this page. B turns to page 83.

SPEAKER A

> **Objectives**
> **Wholesale price per unit**: 200 euros. The retail price will be 250–300 euros, and you want a profit margin of at least 25%.
> **Desks to be supplied per year**: 15,000 units. You think you can sell five a week in each of your 60 stores.
> **Duration of agreement**: Two years. You don't want to commit yourself for much longer.
> **Delivery to begin**: Three months from now. There is a gap in your range, and you need to fill it quickly.
>
> - Before you begin negotiations, look at the points above, and the negotiating expressions in 1–7 and a–g on page 72.
> - Think of the points you are going to make, and how B might react. Prepare five or six expressions that you think you may use.
> - You meet B for the negotiations. Try to use as many of the expressions that you prepared as possible.

2 This is a discussion for two speakers.

A works with another student who had the B role in 2, and B works with another student who had the A role.

Use the expressions in **bold** in a–g on page 72 to explain to your partner what happened in your own negotiation.

3 Write an e-mail summarising what you decided in the role play in Exercise 1. If you were the buyer, write to the salesperson. If you were the salesperson, write to the buyer.

Use these phrases in your e-mail:
It was very nice …
I'm writing to …
We agreed to …
In addition, we agreed to …
I look forward to …

Close appropriately.

Be sure to include details of what you decided about:
- wholesale price per unit
- quantities to be supplied
- the duration of the agreement
- when delivery is to begin

KEY VOCABULARY

Details for agreement

Match the expressions on the left with examples of them on the right.

1	shipping method	A	oak legs and frame, glass top 155 cm × 230 cm
2	specifications	B	by truck
3	order quantity	C	bank transfer in euros
4	method of payment	D	consignments of 100 units
5	discount terms	E	monthly invoices
6	billing	F	5% for annual order quantities over 600,000 euros

1 Ewa Kowalska of Meblopol negotiated with Agneta Dahlquist of Milieu in Stockholm. When she got back to Warsaw, she received this fax from Agneta.

In most of the numbered lines (1–6), there is one extra word that does not fit. One or more lines, however, are correct. If a line is correct, put a tick next to it. If there is an extra word, cross it out.

MILIEU AB

www.milieu.com
Furniture for the world
Box 333, Solna, Stockholm S-170 66, Sweden
Tel +46 (0)8 782 3400, Fax +46 (0)8 782 3450

To: Ewa Kowalska
Sales Director
Meblopol Sp. z. o. o., Warsaw
Fax + 48 22 631 22 99

27 November

Dear Ewa,

It was very nice meeting you last week. I hope you had a pleasant trip back to Warsaw. This is to confirm the key points of our discussion.

1   We agreed to that Meblopol will supply 16,000 desks a year, made to the dimensions
2   and specifications mentioned with on the next page, for an initial period of three years.
3   The wholesale price per unit will be of 215 euros, and delivery is to commence on 1 January.
4   We did not discuss payment conditions during our meeting, but our usual payment terms will
5   apply: you will invoice to us in euros every six months for the desks supplied during that
6   period. We pay for by bank transfer 60 days from receipt of invoice.

If you can confirm that you accept these terms and conditions, I will ask our lawyers to draw up a contract (in Swedish with an English translation) and send it to you by courier.

I very much look forward to doing business with you, and look forward to receiving your confirmation of the above points.

Best regards,

Agneta Dahlquist

Agneta Dahlquist
Chief Buyer, Milieu AB
E-mail: agneta.dahlquist@milieu.com

2 Below is Ewa Kowalska's reply to the above fax. Choose the correct alternative to fill each gap.

MEBLOPOL Sp. z. o. o.

www.meblopol.com ——————
ul. Kolejowa 99,
01-217 Warszawa,
Poland
Tel.+48 22 631 22 00,
Fax +48 22 631 22 99

Agneta Dahlquist
Chief Buyer
Milieu AB, Stockholm

Fax + 46 8 782 3450

28 November

Dear Agneta,

It was a pleasure meeting you last week. The trip back here went very smoothly. Thanks for your fax. Unfortunately, I've checked my notes from the meeting, and I think there has been a misunderstanding on one or two points.

We did agree that Meblopol will supply 16,000 desks a year, made to the dimensions and (1) _____ you mentioned, but my understanding was that this is for an initial period of four years, not three years, with a price per unit of 220 euros, not 215. (2) _____ can commence on 1 January, as you suggest. This is rather (3) _____ for us, but I think we can do it. I agree to the payment (4) _____ you mention.

If you'd like to discuss this on the phone, I'll be here every day this week except Friday. I'm (5) _____ that we can come to an agreement. If you can agree to the above points, our (6) _____ will have a look at the contract that you propose. If you would like us to start delivery in January, we must move quite (7) _____ on this.

Looking forward to hearing from you,

Best wishes,
Ewa Kowalska

Ewa Kowalska

Sales Director
Meblopol Sp. z. o. o.
E-mail: e.kowalska@meblopol.com

---

1 a) specify b) specifics c) specificities d) specifications
2 a) deliver b) delivery c) delivered d) delivers
3 a) tight b) short c) tense d) rapid
4 a) term b) terms c) times d) timely
5 a) confide b) confidential c) confiding d) confident
6 a) lawyers b) legals c) legislators d) legislation
7 a) quick b) quicker c) quickest d) quickly

Role play: Speaker B

June 1: You can't find the invoice on the computer system. Say that you will look into it and get back to A.

June 8: You have found the invoice and put it on the system for payment on June 15.

June 20: There was a computer problem on June 15. Payment will now be made on June 30.

July 6: The cheque was sent and must have got lost in the post. The department head is on holiday until July 31, and you need her authorisation in order to send another one. Apologise but say there is nothing you can do.

You have sent Alvin Palmer's PA a fax with the following information. Unfortunately some of the information was impossible to read. Answer the PA's queries about dates, times and costs.

fax

Option 1

Cost $4,446.15
Business class round trip
▶ MetroJet flight 2784 on a Boeing 737-200
From: Raleigh/Durham, Monday Dec 3, dep 16.10
To: Boston, arr 17.59

Olympic flight 416 on a Boeing 747;
1 stop (in Frankfurt: no change of planes)
From: Boston, Monday Dec 3, dep 21.10
To: Athens, Greece, Tuesday Dec 4, arr 12.55

Cronus Airlines flight 404 on a Boeing 737-400
From: Athens, Greece, Tuesday Dec 4, dep 15.00
To: Khania, Crete, arr 15.45

Option 2

Cost $4,884.20
Business class round trip
▶ American Airlines flight 174 on a Boeing 767
From: Raleigh/Durham, Monday Dec 3, dep 18.45
To: London Gatwick, Tuesday Dec 4, arr 07.25

Virgin Atlantic flight 1002 on an Airbus Industrie A-320
From: London Gatwick, Tuesday Dec 4, dep 12.30
To: Athens, Greece, arr 16.45

Cronus Airlines flight 406 on a Boeing 737-400
From: Athens, Greece, Tuesday Dec 4, dep 18.00
To: Khania, Crete, arr 18.45

UNIT 3

Speaker B   Pair work

1 Gross Domestic Product per head in Hermosa and its neighbours
(bar chart)

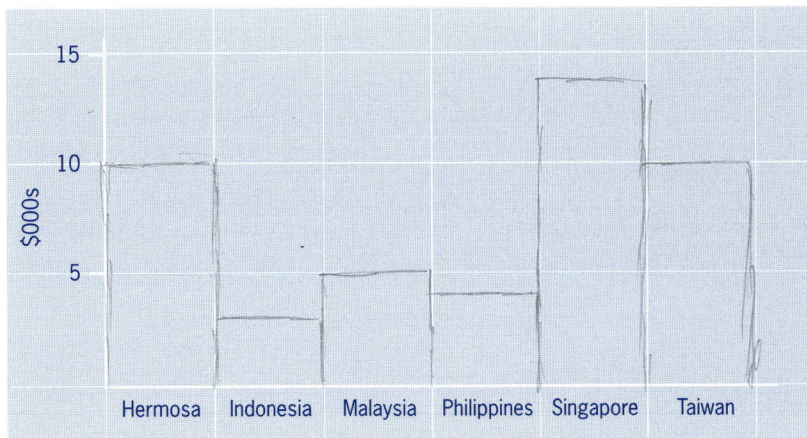

2 Population of Hermosa's major cities: Merida, Vallarta and Newport

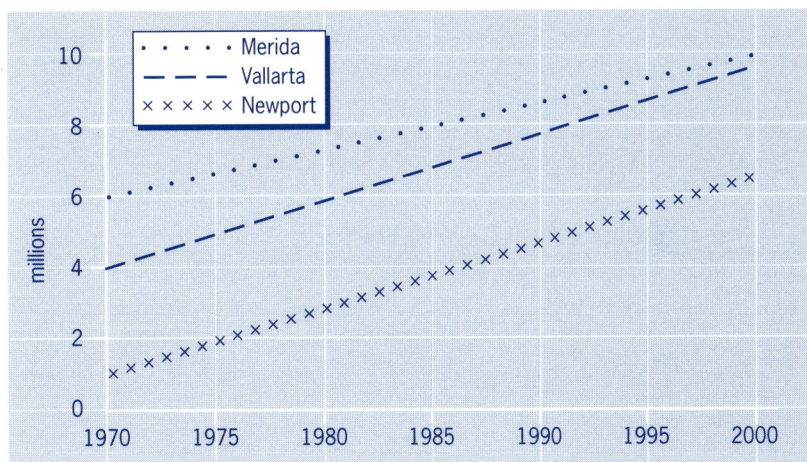

3 Hermosa: cinema visits per person per year
(graph with one line)

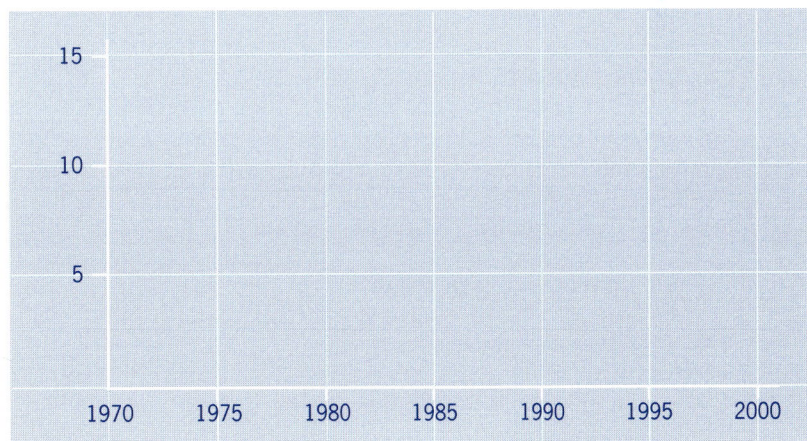

4 Hermosa's workforce

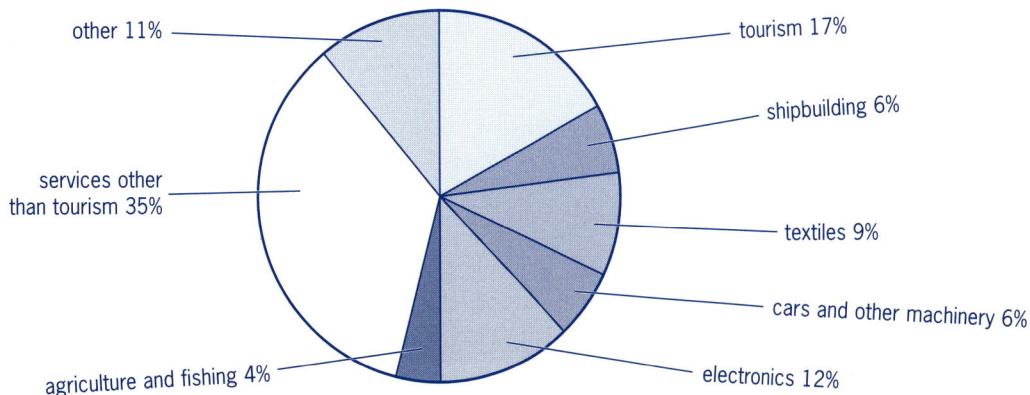

other 11%

tourism 17%

shipbuilding 6%

services other than tourism 35%

textiles 9%

cars and other machinery 6%

agriculture and fishing 4%

electronics 12%

Role play 1

This is your CV. Use the notes below to add to the information in your CV and as a basis for discussion.

> **Nicole Pelissier**
> *1998–present* **Nissan Car Plant, Sunderland, UK. Component Buyer**
> Negotiate terms for supply of car components, including work on programmes for just-in-time delivery and continuous cost reduction. Report to senior management on progress in these areas. Work with engineers on quality control and delivery schedules.
> *1990–98* **Renault plant, Lens, Belgium. Assistant Buyer**
> Helped Buying Manager in planning component orders, contacts with suppliers, etc. Supervised computer analysis of buying costs.
> *1987–90* **HEC (Hautes Etudes Commerciales), Paris**
> Full-time business qualification.
> *1979–85* **Lycée Charlemagne, Paris**
> Baccalauréat C: Maths specialisation.
>
> Good interpersonal skills   Good computer skills
>
> Interests: Chess, golf and computer games, especially chess and golf simulations

- bored with job in Sunderland (present this in a good way)
- would like to move to another industry: very interested in computer industry
- partner is Irish (met in Lens) and would like to move back to Ireland
- attracted by the lifestyle, especially the golf
- left job at Lens after disagreement with Buying Manager about statistical methods of cost analysis (present this in a good way)
- good with all kinds of people: suppliers, production engineers, senior management

Role play 2

This is your CV. Use the notes below to add to the information in your CV and as a basis for discussion.

> **Leslie MacFadden**
> *1993–present* **Trainer, Bell PCs, Dublin**
> One of team of seven trainers at Bell assembly plant. Planning and scheduling of wide range of management and technical courses. Responsible to the Head of Training for quality control and analysis of course outcomes.
> *1987–93* **Physics teacher, Galway High School**
> Gave physics lessons at all levels of school, including leaving certificate level.
> *1986–87* **University College, Galway**
> Trained to teach physics in secondary schools.
> *1983–86* **Midwestern University, Chicago**
> Degree in physics.
> *1981–83* **Lakeside High School, Chicago**
>
> Good interpersonal skills with all levels of employees and management
>
> Interests: baseball, Irish football (amateur player), folk guitar

- you don't work in semiconductors, but in PCs, which use semiconductors, and think change would be easy: physics background means you know about semiconductors, which you read a lot about
- learn new skills fast; anyway, new job involves managing people, rather than knowing content of courses
- want a more senior job and more money
- gave up schoolteaching because fed up with it (but present this in positive way)
- Irish father, Italian mother. Born and grew up in Chicago and moved to Ireland when 21
- single and living alone
- good interpersonal skills with all kinds of people: good relations with current colleagues and boss
- play Irish football for Dublin amateur side, follow US baseball on satellite TV

UNIT 5
SPEAKER B

Entrepreneur	Name of company and base	Product or service	History
Francisco Guerrero	Flyaway, Croydon Airport, near London, UK	Air travel	Founded Flyaway in _____, with money from his father's _____ business in Spain. Started with _____ planes, just _____ routes and _____ staff. Today, more than _____ staff and _____ passengers a year on 15 routes.
Jack Slack	Aston Molecules, Aston Science Park, near Aston University, UK	Pharmaceutical research	Slack was a university teacher of biochemistry. Bought the business from its founder, Malcolm Stevens, another university teacher, in the early 1990s. Slack sold the company in 1996 to US drugs firm OSI, but remained as Managing Director.
_____ _____	_____ _____	Information services	Son graduated from the University of California in San Diego. Worked for _____ in Korea before founding NeoPoint in 1997, developing smart (intelligent) phones and information services. _____ _____ Award, 1999.
Dinu Patriciu	Alpha, Bucharest, Romania	Property, oil refining	After the fall of communism, Patriciu was the first person to register a private company in the country. An architect by training, he got into the property business through the projects he worked on. Now one of the richest people in Romania.
_____ _____	Delance, _____, Switzerland	_____ _____	_____ worked as a _____ in a large _____ company. Asked to produce designs for _____, the designs were not accepted by _____, so she left and set up her own company with her business partner, _____.
Brent Hoberman & Martha Lane Fox	Lastminute.com	Internet service for buying everything from flights to babysitting services	Hoberman, son of Wall Street banker. Lane Fox, daughter of Oxford history professor. Hoberman's father told him business plan would not work. Company now worth several hundred million pounds on paper.

Role play 1

Answer A's questions about the chairs.

Exec	Sten	Soho
Leather covering Available in black or brown Price: 295 euros	Covering looks like leather Available in black Price: 85 euros	Nylon covering Available in red, blue or green Price: 50 euros
Discount for bulk purchases: 10–19 chairs: 5%, 20–49 chairs: 10%, 50 or more: 15% Delivery included for orders over 200 euros, otherwise delivery charge of 20 euros per item		

Useful information:

Sten is now also available in dark blue.

Sten's covering is a new type of plastic that looks very similar to leather.

Both Sten and Soho are very good, long-lasting chairs, but Sten is more modern-looking.

Delivery: Sten 2–3 weeks (currently out of stock); Soho: immediately.

Discount indicated is all you're allowed to give (strict instructions from your boss).

The Exec model is made of real leather. It is only available in black or brown.

Delivery of Exec: 4–6 weeks (has to be made to order).

Say you will talk to your boss about the possibility of a bigger discount.

Role play 2

Respond to A's questions using the following information.
- You have spoken to your boss and you can offer a 25% discount on the Exec chair if A orders at least 75 Sten or Soho chairs.
- If A places a firm order, take the details for delivery.
- The Exec will be delivered later, in ten weeks. (You've had supply problems recently.)
- A can open an account. Payment terms are 30 days from receipt of invoice, which you will arrange to have sent immediately.

UNIT 7
SPEAKER B

Role play 1

A will telephone you. Use these notes as a basis for answering A's questions.

- Three years as an independent installer: relatively successful. Sales of A$1 million per year. Eighty kitchens installed per year. Two employees: Ron and Susan. Very good installers. Get on very well with them. Want to continue working with them.
- Ten years as an installer working for someone else before you started your own business three years ago. You wanted independence, but now want the support of a larger organisation.
- You have A$50,000 capital, but could get more through a bank loan.
- You consider yourself friendly and enjoy dealing with people.

Role play 2

Respond to A's questions by explaining the following:
- your background as an installer and the fact that you now want to open a Smart Kitchens franchise
- you have two people who you can rely on and who you want to continue to work with
- capital required: A$150,000, for showroom and buying stock
- probable turnover: A$100,000–150,000 per month; you think this is realistic
- you already have A$50,000 capital, but you need A$150,000. Can the bank lend A$100,000, to be repaid over five years?
- you can offer your house as security for the loan, but you'd prefer not to, of course

Role play 3

Discuss the loan conditions with A and say that you will call back next week.

UNIT 8
SPEAKER B

Role play 1

You have this information about hotels in and near Khania.

You want to know more about them, and how near they are to the new golf course. Phone A, introduce yourself and obtain the missing information.

Hotel and number of stars	Place	Type	Distance from golf course	Restaurant	Pool	Air-conditioning
Khania Palace****	Ayios Marina			yes	no	yes
Athena****	Khania port			no	yes	yes
Apollo***	Kolimvari			no	yes	no
Helena**	Ayios Marina			yes	no	no

Role play 2

You get three phone calls from potential customers.
Find out what they want and see what you can offer them using the completed information in the table in role play 1.

Role play 1

You want to accept redundancy package.
- You quite like your job as training manager, but there are too many problems.
- Training was the first department to have its budget cut and morale is terrible.
- It's hard to maintain motivation and commitment when morale is so bad.
- You like the lifestyle in Ireland: especially golf, but you miss America, where you grew up.
- You could consider going back there.
- You're looking forward to meeting the outplacement consultants to discuss possibilities.

Role play 2

Below is the latest version of your CV. A will ask you about your time at Random referring to the three headings in the CV:

Recruitment and management of trainers: you enjoyed this, except towards the end, when demand for training went down, trainers' morale suffered and the job became very stressful.

Development of management training: this was extremely interesting. You worked with some important people and the support you got from the company was very good.

Budgets: you liked having this responsibility (until your budget started going down).

You will then talk about the immediate future. You are free to choose between these options:
- stay in Ireland OR go back to US
- look for a similar job OR go back to school teaching OR look for something completely different

Finally, talk about how you see yourself in ten years.
You are completely free to imagine your future!

Leslie MacFadden

2001–present **Head of training, Random Semiconductors**
- recruited and managed team of ten in-house technical trainers
- developed management training with support of senior managers
- responsible for budgets and selection of outside training providers

1993–2001 **Trainer, Bell PCs, Dublin**
One of team of seven trainers at Bell Assembly plant. Planning and scheduling of wide range of management and technical courses.

1987–93 **Physics teacher, Galway High School**
Gave physics lessons at all levels of school, including leaving certificate level.

1986–87 **University College, Galway**
Trained to teach physics in secondary schools.

1983–86 **Midwestern University, Chicago**
Degree in physics.

1981–83 **Lakeside High School, Chicago**

Good interpersonal skills with all levels of employees and management

Interests: baseball, Irish football (amateur player), golf, folk guitar

UNIT 11
SPEAKER B

Ask A questions and complete the information about Uptight Inc.

	Uptight Inc	Laidback Co
Dress		Even the boss wears T-shirts and jeans.
Working hours		No clocking in and out. Company says it judges not on the time worked, but on the results produced. Even so, nobody goes home before 6.30 pm.
Decision-making		Consultation before all decisions. A lot of company meetings with all staff (60 people) present.
Communication		E-mail widely used within the organisation and outside.
Meetings		Meetings take place in company café. Short meetings with people standing, not sitting, are encouraged.
Entertaining		Restaurants considered boring. Boss organises summer barbecues for staff and important clients. Goes sailing with really important clients.

UNIT 12
SPEAKER B

Objectives

Wholesale price per unit: 230 euros. You have calculated that this figure will give you a good profit margin. If you can get more, so much the better. Less than 210 euros, and you will be losing money.

Desks to be supplied per year: At least 17,000 units. You've calculated that Milieu must be able to sell this many worldwide.

Duration of agreement: Preferably four years. In any case, you don't want a shorter agreement than two years.

Delivery to begin: Three months or more from now. This is a complicated new design and you need longer than usual to prepare the machinery, do tests, etc.

- Before you begin negotiations, look at the points above, and the negotiating expressions in 1–7 and a–g on page 72.
- Think of the points you are going to make, and how A might react. Prepare five or six expressions that you think you may use.
- You meet A for the negotiations. Try to use as many of the expressions that you prepared as possible.

Tapescript

UNIT 1 Part A

Exercise 2

A Coca-Cola has its headquarters in Atlanta, Georgia. Coca-Cola is the largest soft drink producer in the world and its products are sold in over 200 countries. It has worldwide sales of $15 billion a year. Products include Coca-Cola Classic, Diet Coca-Cola, Fanta and Sprite. Sales are growing in eastern Europe, the former Soviet Union, China, India and south-east Asia.

B HSBC has its headquarters in London. It is one of the largest banking and financial services organisations in the world. The HSBC Group's international network comprises more than 5,000 offices in 79 countries, operating in the Asia-Pacific region, Europe, the Americas, the Middle East and Africa.

Through a global network linked by advanced technology, the group provides a wide range of personal and commercial financial services. The group has nearly 150,000 employees worldwide.

C Honda was established in 1948 by Soichiro Honda and is today one of the leading makers of cars and the largest manufacturer of motorcycles in the world. The company develops, manufactures, distributes and provides financing for the sale of its motorcycles, automobiles and other products. Honda's manufacturing takes place in 25 separate factories, six of which are located in Japan, five in the United States, two each in Thailand and Brazil and one each in Canada, the United Kingdom, France, Italy, Spain, India, Pakistan, Philippines, Vietnam and Mexico.

Japan accounts for about 28% of sales, North America 52%, Europe 13% and other areas 7%.

D Benetton manufactures and sells clothes and accessories for women, men and children. Accessories include footwear, cosmetics, toys, luggage, watches and leather goods. Manufacturing takes place mostly in Italy, while marketing takes place through a worldwide network of over 7,000 stores, most of which are run on a franchise system. The company has about 8,000 employees of its own, not including franchisees.

Exercises 3 and 4

> I = interviewer
> JS = Jane Smart

I   Jane Smart, you're founder and Chief Executive of Smart Kitchens. Tell us something about how you started the company. Was it easy in the beginning?

JS   I started out in 1979 with a small shop in the centre of Melbourne, not far from our present headquarters. I'd just bought my first flat and had trouble getting a kitchen designed in a way that I liked and thought there must be lots of other people like me, so I decided to start my own company. I took my business plan round to lots of different banks, but it was very difficult getting finance. Eventually I got a bank loan, and we're still with the same bank today.

I   Has the company grown steadily over the years?

JS   I started out with two friends, Rebecca and Jim. They were out installing kitchens while I took care of our little showroom. They're still with the company today as senior managers and major shareholders, and we're still very good friends despite some difficult times. We were all in our late twenties then and we worked incredibly hard to build the company. Now we have 30 showrooms all over the country and 600 employees. I suppose the most difficult time was in the recession of the early nineties. About half of our business is with people who buy kitchens when they move house, and at that time there was a big fall in the number of people moving. We had to lay off some

of our employees and close some of our showrooms. But by the mid nineties, things were on the up again. We were opening more branches and taking on staff again.

I   Are your branches directly owned by the company, or do you work on a franchise system?

JS   We own and run seven of our branch showrooms directly and the rest are franchises. We have a very good relationship with our franchisees. We try to build a relationship of trust with them. If they do things right, they can develop a very profitable business by following our advice. Of course, they benefit from our central buying of materials and equipment, and we pass on cost savings to them. But the main thing is people, and we can give franchisees a lot of assistance in employing the right people and training them. We show our franchisees who to employ, and how to develop their skills, not only on the technical side, but also in management and administration. And we have some very sophisticated computer systems to help them run the business.

I   What advice would you give to someone starting their own business today?

JS   Draw up a realistic business plan – don't be too optimistic about potential sales. Find a bank you can work with – I think things are easier now than they were a few years ago. If you run into financial trouble, keep your bank informed, don't hide things from them. Find the right people, people you can rely on. Employ people you like and that you can get on with – their qualifications may look very good on paper, but it's the human side that's important. And don't underestimate the hours you need to work – at the beginning we were working 80 hours a week. Now it's down to 60, but I enjoy every minute of it.

Exercise 5

1 I'm Rebecca and I started Smart Kitchens with Jane Smart in 1979. For the first few years I did a bit of everything, but now I specialise in developing the number of franchises, dealing with everything from the initial enquiries through to signing the contracts with them.

2 My name's Jim and I've been here with Jane and Rebecca since the beginning. I'm a qualified accountant and I take care of all the financial aspects of running the business, in close collaboration with Jane, of course.

3 Hi, I'm Sandra and I deal with the operations that we run directly in various cities, making sure they have everything they need. I'm on the phone a lot of the day, but things have got easier since we've been using e-mail.

4 I'm Don and I did an architecture degree at Sydney University. I work on the basic kitchen designs that we use. I do a lot of cooking myself at home, trying out various things there.

5 I'm Anna and I work on finding the best suppliers for our kitchen furniture and equipment. We work a lot with the US and Europe, so I'm in contact with companies there quite a lot. I don't have much contact with franchisees, but I do hear eventually if there's some piece of equipment that they like or don't like.

6 My name's Douglas. When franchisees order equipment for installing in their clients' kitchens, I make sure that it's sent to them on time. There are hundreds of different things involved. I only joined the company last week, so please don't ask me too many questions!

UNIT 2 Part B

Exercise 1

A

A   Anna's in the office today but she's on another line. Can I get her to call you?

B   Yes, this is Yvonne Baker at Megabook. She's got my number.

B

C   Hi, you're through to the voicemail of Jerry Salinas. Please leave a message after the tone and I'll get right back to you.

C

D   Oh no, not again. Their switchboard just can't handle the number of calls they get.
E   Yes, I often have the same problem.

D

F   GCDC. Good morning.
G   May I speak to Mr Palmer, please?
F   One moment. I'm putting you through.

E

H   You're through to Megabook Publishing. If you know the extension number you want, enter it now. If you don't know the number, please hold and an operator will be with you shortly.

F

I   Hi, John. It's Dave here again. We were cut off a moment ago.
J   Yeah, there's a problem with my line. It's been like this all week.

Exercises 2 and 3

R = receptionist
AP = Alvin Palmer
SM = Stavros Milatos

R   *Oriste.*
AP   Hello. Can I speak to Mr Milatos, please?
R   May I ask who's calling?
AP   Alvin Palmer.
R   One moment. I'll put you through.
SM   Milatos.
AP   Hi, Stavros, it's Al Palmer. How are you?
SM   Fine, thanks. And you?
AP   Fine. How's the weather over there?
SM   It's a nice warm November day. Perfect for golf!
AP   Great. If we go ahead soon, you'll be playing next November! Did you get our outline proposal?
SM   Yes, I got your e-mail. Looks pretty good. Of course, there are some points we must talk about in more detail.
AP   That's inevitable. But you like the overall idea?
SM   Yes. As you know we've been in touch with a number of companies, but yours is certainly one of the most interesting designs we've seen. How about coming over here to discuss things in the next couple of weeks? And that way you can see the site for yourself. How about the first week of December?
AP   Sounds great. It'll be good if Jerry Salinas, our Technical Director, comes with me. I'll check with him to see if he's free and e-mail you.
SM   Look forward to hearing from you.
AP   It should be in the next couple of days.
SM   It'll be great to see you over here. You can get a direct flight from Athens to Khania and we'll arrange for someone to meet you.
AP   I'm looking forward to seeing Crete. I've never been there. Sounds like a great place.
SM   You'll love it, I'm sure.
AP   OK, my personal assistant will be in touch soon with our arrangements. Bye.
SM   Bye, Al.

Exercise 4

R = receptionist
PA = personal assistant

R   Khania Palace Hotel.
PA   Hello. I'm phoning from a company called GCDC in the United States. I'd like to reserve two rooms from December 4th for three nights, please.
R   Of course. What are the guests' names?
PA   Alvin Palmer, that's P-A-L-M-E-R.
R   P-A-R-M-E-R?
PA   No, P-A-*L*-M-E-R, and Jerry Salinas, S-A-L-I-N-A-S.

R   Salinas. OK, I've got that. About what time will they be arriving?
PA   I don't know yet. Can I confirm that by e-mail? What's your e-mail address?
R   Reception@khaniapalace.gr. That's reception ... at khaniapalace – K-H-A-N-I-A-P-A-L-A-C-E all as one word, dot G-R.
PA   What's the room rate?
R   One hundred and ten euros per night, including breakfast.
PA   I have a special request from Mr Palmer. He is very sensitive to noise. Could you allocate him the quietest room you have?
R   No problem. We'll give him a room on the top floor at the back. There's no noise at all up there, don't worry.
PA   OK. Thanks for your help. I'll be in touch with their exact time of arrival by e-mail.
R   OK. Thank *you* very much. Goodbye.
PA   Bye.

UNIT 3   Part A

Exercise 1

I = interviewer
RC = Rebecca Chu

I   Rebecca Chu is lecturer in Asian Studies at Milton Keynes University. She's a specialist in the economies of south-east Asia, and she's just come back from the island of Hermosa. Rebecca, we don't hear much about Hermosa in this country. Give us a bit of background.
RC   Well, it's a fairly mountainous island in the western Pacific, about 500 kilometres from the Chinese mainland. It was colonised by the Spanish in the seventeenth century and gained independence from Spain in 1898. Nowadays, native Hermosans form about 40% of the population of 40 million and Hispanics, people of Spanish origin, form about 30%. There's a big Chinese community: about 20% of the population is of Chinese origin. Indians make up 6% and other groups form the remaining 4%.
I   Sounds quite a cosmopolitan sort of place.
RC   Yes, the main languages are Spanish, Chinese and Hindi, with English being used more and more, especially for business purposes, as it is in a lot of places, of course.
I   I know Hermosa was one of the boom economies of Asia: one of the Asian Tigers, but didn't it go through a bit of economic difficulty a few years ago, like some of the other Tigers?
RC   Yes, it did, but it was not as badly affected as some of its neighbours, and I think now the boom times have returned. Growth this year looks as though it will be around 5–6%, not the 9% we saw a few years ago but pretty good even so. Unemployment is falling and has returned to the levels of a few years ago: 4% or so, not bad. Inflation is under control at 3% per year, having reached 10% a couple of years ago. Average inflation for the last five years has been 5%. All this is reflected in the exchange rate against the US dollar. For a long time during the 1990s there were about twelve Hermosan pesos to the dollar. Then it went to 30 pesos at the worst point in the economic crisis, but now we're back at what seems a fairly stable rate of 22 pesos to the dollar.
I   What are the main economic activities?
RC   Well, the economy is changing quite fast. They've moved away from the old activities of shipbuilding and textiles, which are no longer very important. New sectors such as electronics are emerging: Hermosa is now one of the world's main centres for the manufacture of personal computers. The real money-spinners in the future are going to be electronics and tourism.
I   Tourism? Hermosa isn't a destination you see much in the travel agencies over here.
RC   No, it's a closely guarded secret, but the beaches on the west coast are fabulous, and they're hoping to open up the area. In fact I spent the last couple of days on my latest trip researching the tourist industry on the west coast, lying on the beach, eating the delicious seafood they've got there. There's a lot of potential, I can tell you!
I   Rebecca Chu, thank you very much.
RC   Thank you.

85

Exercise 3

A   In 1970, Hermosa was beginning to industrialise, but it was still extremely poor, with GDP per head of $900. By 1980, this had reached $1,900 and by 1990, $4,000. The really rapid growth was during the 1990s, with a slight pause in 1997 to 1998, when GDP per head actually fell by 5%, but in 2000, it reached the level of $10,000.

B   There have been big improvements in public health in the period 1970 to 2000 and people in Hermosa are living longer. In 1970, average life expectancy was just 50 years. By 1980, this had reached 56 years, and by 1990, 61 years. Life expectancy in 2000 was 65 years.

C   In 1970, only 45% of the adult population could read and write. But the government realised that a literate workforce was key to economic success, and put a lot of money and effort into education. This began to pay off by 1980, by which time literacy rates had reached about 70%. By 1990, 95% of the adult population could be considered literate. Now illiteracy has been almost wiped out, with 99% of the adult population able to read and write.

D   The roads in Hermosa are getting pretty crowded, that's for sure! On my last trip, I almost missed my plane back as the traffic was so bad getting to the airport. There are now 30 cars per 100 people, almost up to the level of European countries like Spain. Even back in 1990, there were still only 19 cars per 100 people, and not many new roads have been built since then. In 1980, there had been twelve cars per 100 people and, ten years before that, only eight.

E   The first television programmes were broadcast in 1970. At that time there were twelve people per television set. By 1985, this had gone down to about seven people per set. More and more TV channels became available and by 1990 there were six people per set. Today there are four people per set. Hermosans are great watchers of TV and this trend seems likely to continue!

UNIT 4   Part C

Exercise 1

A   You're going to have to take it round the back. This entrance is for visitors only.

B   Excuse me! Where do you think *you're* going?

C   Have you signed in, sir? I can't see your badge.

D   Would you mind putting that cigarette out, sir? Can't you see the sign?

E   No pictures, I'm afraid, madam. I'm going to have to ask you to let me have your film.

F   This is the most confidential area of the plant. You need special clothing to go in, and in any case, it's only open to authorised personnel. Our most closely guarded industrial secrets are in there!

Exercises 2 and 3

Good afternoon, ladies and gentlemen, and welcome to the Random Semiconductors manufacturing plant. As you can see, we're in the reception area. The plant was finished earlier this year, under budget and ahead of schedule. It's the result of a 1.6 billion euro investment.

If you follow me, we'll make our way to the research and development laboratories.

We have some very advanced work going on here, and we can't show you all of it, but as you can see through the window, they're testing new ways of making chips from silicon, the basic raw material in this industry. The chips are used not only in personal computers, but in mobile phones, televisions, every imaginable sort of household and industrial equipment. About 50 R and D staff work here.

This way, please. We're going to cross into the building opposite.

Here we have the company gym. We believe very much in a healthy environment for our employees, and if you join us, you'll have full use of these facilities at no cost. At lunchtime it gets pretty full, I can tell you. We also have a policy of no smoking on the premises, and no alcohol, but as you'll see, there's no shortage of machines for coffee and soft drinks.

Now, if you follow me, please, we'll go back to the main building.

Well, here we are back in the main building, and this is the training centre. It's where most of you will start your career at

Random if you join us. We'll introduce you to the company and to the company culture and show you some of the techniques we use, which may not be what you've seen elsewhere.

Next door we have the production area. You need special clothing to go in, and in any case, it's only open to authorised personnel. Our most closely guarded industrial secrets are in there! But I can tell you that we had a few problems in the beginning, that's quite normal, but now we're just reaching maximum production levels.

Here, you can see the packing area and the bays for trucks to take the goods away. Most of them are taken to Dublin airport for delivery worldwide.

We'll end the tour in the canteen here. My colleagues from recruitment are here, and if you have any questions about working here, I'm sure they'll be happy to answer them. Thank you.

UNIT 5   Part A

Exercises 1 and 2

1   I've just flown down from Aberdeen. I was up there to do some consultancy work for an oil company. My client is paying for the trip, but they'll be very pleased when I send in my bill – I only paid £35 one-way. Am I satisfied with Flyaway? Yes, very. I'd give it nine out of ten.

2   I'm going to see my daughter who lives in Madrid. She's just had a baby, my first grandchild! I wouldn't have been able to afford the fare before, but with Flyaway it costs just £52 one way. Obviously I haven't been on the plane yet, but my impressions of the airline are very good. The girl who sold me the ticket on the phone was very sweet and the check-in staff have been extremely pleasant. I'd give it eight.

3   I'm Production Manager for a car company. We've just been bought by a German company and I'm off to Frankfurt to meet some of my new colleagues. My company are only paying £70 for this trip. *[Last call for flight FA234 to Frankfurt. Would all remaining passengers please proceed to Gate 5 immediately.]* That's my flight! Must rush!

4   I've just arrived from Stockholm. I've just started my own company, three employees including me, so I'm very conscious of costs. This flight was very cheap compared to the other airlines on the route, and we arrived ahead of schedule, which is unusual these days. Flyaway are great. OK, the sandwiches on the plane are not terrific, but I'm not looking for a gastronomic experience, I just want to get from A to B as efficiently as possible. I give them ten out of ten!

5   I'm studying for a degree in Italian at the University of Croydon, but this year I'm doing my year abroad in Milan. I live near Croydon, so this airport is very convenient. I've just been home for the weekend to see my parents. I can afford to because it's so cheap, only £37 one-way. I give them eight out of ten. I'd really recommend Flyaway to anybody.

6   When you're unemployed like me, it's good to get away for a few days. I've just been for a week's holiday down in Malaga in Spain. Fantastic place. Couldn't afford to go there normally, but Flyaway's fares are so cheap. This bloke Guerrero, I think that's his name, you know, the guy who started the airline, he's doing a really good job. He gets my vote any day. Seven out of ten, that's pretty good on my scale.

Exercises 3 and 4

> P = presenter
> FG = Francisco Guerrero

P   On tonight's programme we have Francisco Guerrero, founder of Flyaway, the low-cost airline, recently voted Low-Cost Airline of the Year. Mr Guerrero, can I start by asking you why you started Flyaway? Aren't there enough airlines in Europe already?

FG   There are a lot of airlines, government-owned and independent, but mentally they're stuck in an age when flying was seen as an exclusive luxury. When you fly on some of the national airlines, you get the feeling they are run more for the benefit of their employees than the passengers. Even if some of these airlines have been privatised, the mentality is still the same. They're just a cartel, all charging basically the same high fares. There's no real competition. We wanted to change all that with services that get you from A to B safely and punctually for a reasonable amount of money.

P How do you keep your costs down?

FG We sell direct to the public over the phone and on the internet, so we cut out the travel agents. We don't have luxurious offices in the centre of London, and we don't issue tickets, we just give a confirmation number that people give to our staff when they check in. And, of course, we don't serve meals on the plane. Passengers can buy sandwiches and coffee if they want to, but they don't expect free meals. And we have only one type of plane, which reduces maintenance costs.

P You're based at Croydon airport outside London, not one of the big airports. Isn't that a disadvantage?

FG No, you can get to it by train more quickly than to Gatwick. Checking in is quick and it's a two-minute walk to the plane. Delays are rare because we're the only big airline using the airport. That's one of the reasons we've grown so quickly – people know there won't be queues and delays.

P You're buying one new plane a month. Isn't that risky, given the unpredictable nature of the airline industry? In an economic turndown, isn't air travel usually one of the first things to be affected?

FG No, we believe that, because of lower fares, air travel will be a necessity for ordinary people, rather than a luxury. They'll go on travelling even if there is a recession.

P How do you see the European airline industry ten years from now?

FG Well, deregulation will continue but some of the national airlines will still be receiving money from their governments. Studies show that the market for air travel in Europe will nearly have doubled. Deregulation will mean that a lot of new airlines will be starting up, especially in countries where the national airline has more or less had a monopoly. Some independent airlines will have gone out of business, unfortunately, because they will have been unable to control their costs.

P And where do you see Flyaway in all this?

FG Well, obviously I hope that we will be one of the market leaders in European air travel. We started five years ago with two planes, just two routes and 40 staff. Today we have more than 900 staff and four million passengers a year on 15 routes. Obviously we would like to see that growth continue.

P Well, thank you for talking to us, and good luck with your plans.

FG Thank you very much.

UNIT 6   Part A

Exercise 1

1 I'm out on the road most of the time, so I don't use my desk in the office very much. In fact, I don't really need one at all, but it's nice to have a base I can come back to in the office. There's never anything on my desk as I have everything I need on my laptop computer. I share my desk with a colleague but he's never there either. It has some sort of grey plastic covering, I think. So we just have one of those basic office desks you see in office furniture catalogues, and a basic black plastic-covered chair, but people are always "borrowing" the chair. The other salespeople have the same thing. There's a sales meeting every Monday morning, but otherwise we're never here.

2 I like to have a very large desk made of some rare tropical wood – I know it's illegal now but I did manage to get one – don't ask me how. It's just that I don't like modern materials at all – they look so cheap. I keep my desk completely clear of papers. There's just a telephone on my desk. There's a computer in the next room, but only my personal assistant uses it. I'm head of the organisation and I don't believe in all this democratic stuff. When people come into my office I like them to feel slightly nervous. They have quite a long way to walk and when they sit down, they're much lower than me. My own chair is made of black leather and it has a very high back.

3 As office manager, I never leave the office and I spend 45 hours a week at my desk, so I like to make things comfortable. My desk isn't large – I think it's made of wood, but I haven't seen the surface of the top of my desk for some time – it's always covered with papers and

files and half-empty coffee cups. People think I'm messy and disorganised, but *I* know exactly where everything is all the time. I have a PC, of course, and this takes up quite a lot of desk-space. I could just keep everything on the computer, but I like printing things out and seeing them on paper. Of course, that makes more stuff to put on my desk. The chair is red and made of some sort of fabric; it might be cotton but it's probably synthetic. Nice to have a bit of colour – most office furniture is grey or black.

4 I like a sense of light in my office, so I have a desk with a transparent glass top. I have a rather strange-looking chair, strange if you haven't seen one before. I'm a secretary and I do a lot of typing and this chair is designed for that – the chair has two parts and you sort of kneel and sit forward at the same time. The idea is that you avoid getting problems in your back and your neck. Anyway, back to the desk. I don't like things to get disorganised. I always put papers and files into neat piles on my desk, otherwise I find my thinking gets confused!

5 I'm a graphic designer – I do the designs for packaging, book covers, that sort of thing. I worked in offices for 20 years. I hate modern offices, the lighting is terrible, the furniture is ugly. I wanted to get away from that completely. I'm self-employed now, and I work at home. Luckily, I've got a spare room I can use as an office. In there I've got one of those large old-fashioned wooden tables. I work on a computer with a very large screen, and there's a coffee machine nearby, with unlimited supplies of coffee – essential for work!

6 Yeah, well here we don't want people to feel they "own" a particular desk. They take whatever's available when they arrive in the morning, connect their laptop computer to the company network and start working. I'm in advertising and many of us are out seeing clients a lot of the time. And we have a lot of meetings so people are away from their desks most of the time anyway. We try to make the meetings as short as possible, so we have no chairs in the meeting rooms. We stand around a long, narrow, high table and try to get things done as quickly as possible!

Exercise 2

People spend 40 hours a week or more in their offices, but it's strange how little we think about the design of the ideal working environment. A lot of modern offices are far from ideal. Glass buildings may look good from the outside, but when the sun starts shining the temperature inside can go up very quickly, however good the air-conditioning is. It's very frustrating to feel you can't open a window, and this gives you the feeling of being "trapped" in the building.

Then there's the question of lighting. There's something about modern strip lighting, you know, those long tubes, that's very tiring on the eyes. Studies have shown that this can have a dramatic effect on productivity – people get headaches and problems with their eyesight and of course their work suffers. My advice is to work in natural daylight, but of course this is not always possible.

And of course another problem for your eyes is computer screens. You can adjust the brightness and so on, but long hours in front of the screen can be very bad for the eyes. So I suggest that people vary their activities and get up and walk around to do something else at least once an hour, but again that's not always possible when you're working to tight deadlines.

The screen should be positioned so that it's at or below eye level. It shouldn't be somewhere where you have to look up at it, so your desk should be the right height. You should use a chair that gives good support to your lower back, and you should sit up straight with your elbows hanging naturally at your side. There should be space in front of your keyboard to put your hands. Your thighs should be horizontal, with your feet solidly on the floor so that the weight of your legs is on your feet. You should use something to rest your feet on if necessary.

A lot of people work in an open-plan environment in one very large room, with partitions between desks, instead of having their own office. Working with so many people around you can be very difficult. The phones are ringing all the time, and other people's phone conversations can be very distracting and tiring. There seem to be constant interruptions where people come and ask you questions about things that have nothing to do with you.

Perhaps it's not surprising that home working is getting more popular. This is what we call telecommuting. With modern technology – e-mail, internet and so on – for a lot of people, it doesn't really matter where they work, as long as they produce results. A lot of managers still don't like the idea of not seeing the people that they supervise, but home working will certainly take off in the years to come. If you work at home you should try to have a properly equipped room where you work, where you can set up your computer properly in the way I mentioned earlier. That way you can close the door when you've finished work for the day. A lot of people working from home complain that there's no clear dividing line between work and family – this is one way of "switching off" from work.

UNIT 7 Part C

Exercises 1 and 2

> C = customer
> F = franchisee

1

C Hello, your people installed a kitchen in my flat last week, and everything's fine except the oven – I can't seem to make it work. Are you sure it's connected OK?

F Yes, they're a bit difficult to operate, those ovens. There's a switch that's rather difficult to see, on the left hand side. You've got to switch that on first.

2

C My name's Laver and I'm phoning because I've been waiting for you to arrive all morning to start work on the kitchen I ordered. What's going on?

F Ah, Mr Laver, I think there's been a misunderstanding. If you check carefully, you'll find that we said next Monday, not this Monday. It was in the letter we sent you confirming your order. Yes, I've got a copy of the letter on my screen in front of me: Monday the 22nd, we said, not the 15th.

3

C Your people were here installing a kitchen this morning. They took all the old equipment away: the fridge, the old oven and so on but they left it in my neighbour's parking space in front of the building. When my neighbour gets in this evening, she's going to be very angry.

F Don't worry. The guys are going to come and take it away in the next hour. It's a different team who deal with the old equipment. I'll call them on the mobile and make sure they get to you as quickly as they can.

4

C The kitchen you installed last week looks great, but I'm having trouble with the fridge. It's very cold inside the main compartment, and everything's frozen, not in the freezer, I mean, but in the main part of the fridge. The beer's completely frozen.

F If you look in the instruction manual, you'll see the required settings. Just try turning it down a bit.

5

C Jessica James here. I've received the bill for the work you did, but I don't understand the calculations. The price you gave me originally was $12,000, but the invoice is for nearly $20,000.

F Just a moment. Let me just find a copy of the invoice. The price of $12,000 we quoted was for equipment and materials. If you take a closer look, I think you'll find that on the second page of the quote, you'll see a figure for the labour, bringing the total up to $19,328.

Exercises 3 and 4

> I = interviewer
> BE = bank executive

I How long have you been working in the loans area?

BE I've been in this department for ten years and I've seen some very interesting business projects in that time. I wouldn't say they were all good, but interesting, yes, definitely.

I What are your criteria for deciding if a project is good or not?

BE Well, with companies that are already in existence, we look at the background of the company. Personal contact is very important. A lot of the applicants have been banking with us for years, and we look back to see what sort of history they have with us. Have their company's accounts with the bank been in credit all that time, or have they been in a situation where they spend more than there is in the account without arranging it with the bank first? And we look at their clients to see if *they* are paying on time, and so on.

I And what about people who want to start a business from scratch?

BE Well again, if they're already personal clients at the bank we look back to see if their personal finances have been in order, or if they've had a lot of overdrafts. We think that if someone can't keep their own finances in order, they may have trouble running the finances of a small business.

I But what about the business ideas themselves? How do you decide if they are any good?

BE Well, as I say, we see a lot of them, and of course we don't know everything about every type of business. But it is important that they have a good, realistic business plan.

I What do you mean by realistic?

BE Well, that's the $64,000 question. People can be over-optimistic. They underestimate the costs and overestimate the potential sales, especially for the first few months of operation. Part of our job is to bring them back down to earth and point out how it might take years to build up a reasonable level of business activity. And meanwhile, the costs are there, the office, the heating, salaries, repayments on loans are going out even if the company isn't selling anything. So we don't pretend to know about every type of business, but we do take a close look at the business plan to see if it's similar to business plans we've seen in the past, ones we know that have worked.

I How do you react when people say that banks don't do enough to encourage small businesses, and that these businesses are limited in their growth by the attitudes of banks who refuse to lend them money?

BE As I say, we study all the business plans that we receive very carefully. Of course, we'd like to make as much money as possible by lending as much as possible. But we know that some of the projects are not going to work and that we will make some loans that are not repaid. But we have to be very sure that there aren't too many loans like this. You have to remember that a bank is a business as well, not a charity. We have to make money. And, among other things, this means limiting the losses on bad loans as much as possible.

UNIT 8 Part A

Exercise 1

> SM = Stavros Milatos
> AP = Alvin Palmer
> JS = Jerry Salinas

SM Alvin, hello, very nice to meet you.

AP Very good to meet *you*, Stavros. Let me introduce our Technical Director, Jerry Salinas.

JS Hello.

SM Good to meet you. Did you have a good flight?

JS Everything went very smoothly. No delays anywhere.

SM Good. How's your hotel?

AP Comfortable and very quiet. I think I've slept off my jetlag already!

SM Yes. The Khania Palace has got a very good reputation. In fact, it's owned by my brother-in-law.

AP Really!

SM Let's go up to my office.

Exercise 2

1 This project is way behind schedule. We underestimated the preparation required before we could start building. We should have reached roof level by now, but we're still only on the 18th floor!

2 We'll be landing in Barcelona in about 20 minutes, right on schedule. We've had the benefit of the wind behind us, so we've made up some of the time we lost at Heathrow before takeoff.

3 The exam's in a month, but we've got rather behind with the programme. We'll just have to cover the last part of the course in record time, and let's hope there aren't any questions about it in the exam!

4 The program has taken us less time to write than we'd anticipated. This is unusual, I admit, but we'll be able to start testing the software next week, a month ahead of the original schedule.

5 It was very slow writing the first chapter, but things are going much faster now. I know it was supposed to be ready by this week, but I should be able to make up lost time and let you have the manuscript in two months. Is that OK?

Exercise 3

SM = Stavros Milatos
JS = Jerry Salinas

JS We've used the photographs and maps that you sent us to prepare some basic plans, but we'll need another month or so to finalise them.

SM That's fine. Meanwhile, we'll get estimates from some local building firms for laying out the course itself and the building construction work: the clubhouse, the access roads, the car park and so on. That should take a couple of months, so we'd be able to start in February.

JS Obviously the course can be laid out and the buildings constructed at the same time.

SM What about the watering system?

JS Of course, the pipes for watering the grass would be put in before we lay the grass, that's logical. The pipe system usually takes a month or so to install, and we would do that in February before beginning construction of the main part of the course, which would last from March to the end of September.

SM How about laying the grass?

JS Good point. We would do that at the end of the summer, in October, to avoid the heat. I guess it gets pretty hot here in July and August!

SM It certainly does! In the summer 40, even 45 degrees is quite common, especially in the last few years. And what sort of lead-time are we looking at for the construction of buildings, access roads and so on?

JS About seven months, from February to the end of August, plus two more months for the finishing touches: painting the inside of the clubhouse, installing furniture and so on. If we do start in February, you could open in November, just in time for the winter golf season.

SM We're going to have to. The course is in next year's tourist brochures already!

UNIT 9 Part A

Exercise 1

1 The biggest merger in corporate history was announced yesterday when the internet service provider Connect said that it was to join forces with the media company Globalmedia. The merger will produce the biggest media company in the world, allowing Globalmedia to distribute its films and other content to Connect's 20 million subscribers.

2 The yen rose against the US dollar to close at 95.6 yen to the dollar. The euro again fell below the psychologically important barrier of one euro to one dollar, to close at 99.5 US cents. In Asia, the Hermosan peso came under pressure, falling at one point to 25 pesos to the US dollar.

3 In France, protesters blocked construction of a new motorway bridge that will be the biggest in Europe by sitting in front of earth-moving machinery for three hours. They were removed by police, who made three arrests. A local politician described the protesters as "environmental extremists" and said that by their actions they were "damaging the future of the regional economy".

4 The number of people out of work has fallen to its lowest level for 25 years. Businesses in some areas say that it is now almost impossible to find the staff they require. Job centres in some cities in the prosperous south report that unemployment is effectively zero. But the picture across the country is uneven, with some job centres in northern cities reporting that long-term unemployment there is on the increase.

5 There will be a one-day stoppage next Monday by train drivers in the south-west region protesting against new working practices and pay scales. Services are likely to be disrupted and travellers are advised to call 0800 484 985 before setting out on their journey.

Exercise 2

N = newsreader
KS = Kate Simpson
ST = Susie Tan

N There has been a night of rioting in the Hermosan city of Puerto Escondido. Rioters were protesting against the construction of an oil refinery near the city, centre of one of the country's main tourist areas. Our correspondent Kate Simpson is in Puerto Escondido. Kate, what's the latest situation there?

KS Well, Peter, what began yesterday morning as a peaceful demonstration against the building of the oil refinery had turned violent by yesterday evening, with some demonstrators confronting the police and throwing stones and bottles. About 20 cars were set on fire and some buildings were looted. I saw demonstrators taking televisions and other electrical goods from shops, and food from supermarkets.

N Some people are saying that the authorities over-reacted to what, in the beginning, was a peaceful demonstration. Can you confirm that?

KS Well, yesterday afternoon there were certainly a lot of police out on the streets, but things looked reasonably calm, with demonstrators peacefully carrying banners and shouting slogans. This is a small town, and a lot of people had come in by bus from other cities in Hermosa. Among them were what the mayor here, Susie Tan, called "trouble-makers". This is what she said about the protests last night.

ST Puerto Escondido is usually a very peaceful place. Of course, it's a free country and everybody has the right to express their point of view, but I think the demonstrators should remember that investment is necessary for this country's future.

KS The situation is now tense but calm here. We'll only get a complete picture of the number of people injured and damage to property in the morning. But meanwhile, one thing is certain – environmental protest here, as in many other places around the world, has become more confrontational and violent. Now back to the studio in London.

Exercise 3

N = newsreader
RC = Rebecca Chu

N I'm joined now by Rebecca Chu, lecturer in Asian Studies at Milton Keynes University, and a specialist in Hermosan affairs. Rebecca Chu, those were pretty angry scenes we saw there. What's the background to this rioting?

RC Well, Peter, since the construction of the oil refinery was announced last year, there has been mounting anger against the project. Green Action, the environmental organisation, has co-ordinated demonstrations all around the country, including this latest one, and activists have occupied the site of the proposed refinery on the coast, about ten kilometres north of Puerto Escondido. The head of Green Action in Hermosa says they will stay there as long as necessary, until the refinery project is cancelled.

N What's the government's position on the refinery? Have they moved at all following the protests?

RC Well, they continue to say that the refinery is absolutely essential for the development of the economy. The Ministry of Industry says that this site is the only place the refinery can be built. They say that if Hermosans want to go on enjoying higher living standards, they have to accept projects like this.

N I understand this is a potentially important area for tourism in the future.

RC Well, tourism is certainly an important part of the Hermosan economy, even if the west coast has not been developed yet. But it's the big industrial infrastructure projects that are seen as more important than everything else. Of course, tourism is the world's biggest industry, but a lot of countries see tourism as somehow not serious. Big industrial projects are treated by the governments of developing countries with much more respect.

N Rebecca Chu, thank you very much for joining us.

UNIT 10 Part A

Exercise 1

1 Demand for cars has been growing strongly recently, especially in Germany and France. Consumers in those countries are less worried about the economic outlook and are spending more freely. Sales last month were up by 6.5% on the same period a year ago.

2 After a long period of increasing ticket sales, trips to the cinema are currently declining. There have been fewer big film releases this year. And there is a long-term decrease in the number of people between 12 and 25, who make up a large part of the movie-going audience.

3 Pig farmers in Britain have seen a 30% decline in prices since last year. There is increasing competition in pork and pork products from abroad, and the overall market is getting smaller, with people eating less and less meat in general. Pig farmers in Britain have been going out of business at the rate of 50 per week.

4 Clothing sales in the newly industrialised economies of Asia have been very strong in the last six months. All the big international chains such as Benetton and Marks and Spencer have reported record sales there, in some places 20% up on the same period last year. Growth has been especially strong in the haute couture sector.

5 Personal computer manufacturers have been used to annual growth rates of 10 to 12% in the last few years, but no longer. Global demand for PCs last year was 5% lower than in the previous year. Suppliers to the PC market, such as the chip makers who produce key computer components, have begun to feel the effects of this downturn.

Exercise 2

P = presenter
RA = Robyn Ashley

P Three years ago hi-tech businesses around Dublin were booming. Among the newcomers was Random Semiconductors, who built a 1.6 billion euro plant and research centre here. But there have been rumours of cutbacks, and this week came the news that many had been fearing. Random is to halve production at the plant, and transfer all its research and development to its American research centre. Robyn Ashley is a specialist on employment in the semiconductor industry and she's with me in the studio. Robyn: bad news, but not entirely unexpected, I think.

RA That's right, Peter. The downturn in PC sales last year seems to have been a turning point in the industry. Everybody who was going to buy a personal computer has now bought one, and people and companies who already have PCs are not replacing them at the same rate as before. Internet access is now the main application for a PC, and you can now get internet access in cheaper and easier ways than through a personal computer. Of course, at the heart of every PC are the processors made by companies like Random Semiconductors.

P But don't Random also make processors for other products like mobile phones?

RA That's right, but 70% of their production was for the PC industry, and, as you were saying, they've decided to halve production at the plant and transfer R and D elsewhere.

They're not leaving Ireland completely, and they may increase production again and bring back R and D if there's a turnaround in the PC market, but for the moment there's overcapacity in the global semiconductor market, with too many companies fighting over smaller and smaller demand, at least in the short-term.

P What effect will it have on the local economy?

RA Well, Random is going to have to let a lot of people go. Random say they will try to make the cuts through voluntary redundancies and natural wastage, but I'd say they're going to have to make some compulsory redundancies too, especially on the research side. These people may find work in other companies, but other companies in the region have similar problems, and they may have to look elsewhere for work.

P What about jobs in other companies?

RA Of course, cutbacks like this affect the whole local economy, not just employees of the company. They affect Random's suppliers, of course, suppliers of everything from advanced components to delivery services. A lot of companies have set up business in the same area as Random and other large companies, knowing they will be an important source of work. And then there's the local housing market, with houses of former employees all going on the market at the same time. Think of the local supermarkets, with fewer customers and less money to spend. The list is endless.

UNIT 11 Part A

Exercise 1

1 Pierre Martin here, that's M-A-R-T-I-N, from the *Geneva Business Daily*, an English language business paper in Geneva – I'm sure you've heard of it. I'm a reporter on the paper. I'm calling to see if it would be possible to arrange an interview to discuss the takeover of White Cross Airways – our readers will be very interested, I'm sure. I'm going to be in London next week on Monday and Tuesday. We could meet somewhere in central London, or I could come out to your offices at Croydon airport. Please could you contact me on 00 41 22 769 4341. Thank you.

2 Suzanne Byers here at Clifton Lansdown. The legal documents are almost all completed in connection with the takeover, but there are one or two small details to clarify. I'd be grateful if Mr Guerrero could call me at home this evening on 01865 508318. Any time until midnight would be fine as this is rather urgent. Thank you so much.

3 This is Brian Jack at the *Financial Press*. We'd like to do an interview with Francisco Guerrero about the White Cross takeover. We could send someone down to Croydon any day this week. Could someone give me a call on 020 7908 3529? Thanks.

4 Hey, Francisco! It's Joe. Great news on the deal! I knew you'd do it. How about a game of tennis and a beer to celebrate! Tomorrow, Tuesday would be great. See you at the Country Club at six? Bye for now!

5 This is Marie-Claire Allain at White Cross in Geneva. I'm glad the takeover talks went so well. I'm really looking forward to working with you in our new combined operation. I'm going to be in London next Wednesday. How about lunch at the Savoy, say at one o'clock? Now that all the financial detail of the takeover is clear, it'll be good to talk more about strategy.

Exercises 2 and 3

I = interviewer
FG = Francisco Guerrero

I So, Mr Guerrero, can you tell us why you've bought White Cross Airways? Isn't it making quite large losses? Wasn't there a loss last year of seven million Swiss francs on sales of 100 million?

FG Yes, but we hope to turn that situation round quite quickly. As you know, White Cross is based at Geneva, and they have ten routes such as Geneva–Barcelona, Geneva–Copenhagen and so on. I'm sure these can be developed if we offer low-cost, basic services like the ones we offer on Flyaway – no meals, just coffee that passengers pay for, that sort of thing. Several million people live within two hours of Geneva in Switzerland and France – it's not very far from Lyon, you know, and all these people are potential customers. If we can offer low-cost flights, I'm sure we can develop this market.

I   Why did you choose an airline in Switzerland rather than somewhere else? Looking at the research, I see there are three or four loss-making airlines in western Europe that could be potential takeover targets.

FG   Well, Geneva is an underused airport with lots of room for expansion, and it's a central location in Europe. We hope to develop Geneva as a European hub.

I   In what ways?

FG   Well, passengers would fly to Geneva and change planes there. It will allow us to offer destinations that otherwise would not be profitable on direct flights to Europe. We have nineteen direct flights at the moment, flying from Croydon airport near London. So, for example, someone could fly to Geneva and then take a connecting flight to somewhere else, such as Sofia, you know, Sofia in Bulgaria. It might not be profitable for us to offer London to Sofia direct, but with people coming in on other flights from other parts of Europe, they can change planes in Geneva and get on the flight to Sofia.

I   You say Geneva has lots of room for expansion. How do you mean?

FG   Well, to give you an idea, last year seven million passengers went through Geneva. Over 60 million went through Heathrow, the main London airport. One hundred and sixty thousand planes took off and landed in Geneva, 450,000 flights at Heathrow. I'm not saying we want to make Geneva like Heathrow, but there is a lot of room in Geneva for more passengers and more flights.

I   Do you have plans for more acquisitions? Do you have your eyes on other prey?

FG   Let's see how this one goes first. But it's no secret that it would be good to get into the transatlantic market one day.

I   What about the national airlines? How are they reacting to all this?

FG   As usual, they're complaining and talking about unfair competition and so on. They haven't changed.

UNIT 12   Part A

Exercises 1 and 2

EK = Ewa Kowalska
IJ = Ingvar Jonsson

EK   Excuse me. That copy of the *Financial Press*. Could I have a look at it if you've finished with it?

IJ   Yes, of course. Not much in it today though.

EK   Excuse me. But aren't you Ingvar Jonsson, founder of the Milieu furniture chain?

IJ   That's right. How did you recognise me? I try to keep a low profile!

EK   I saw a photograph of you in a furniture trade magazine last week – you know, *Furniture World*. I thought it was you. I really admire what you've done, bringing good design to ordinary people. I see Milieu opened another store in Poland last week, in Krakow wasn't it?

IJ   Yes. That's right. It's our third store in Poland. I've just been down there to see how things are going. We're a big organisation now, but I like to see things with my own eyes, talk to employees and customers. That's the only way to know what's really going on. I guess you're in the furniture business if you read the trade magazines!

EK   Yes. My name's Ewa Kowalska. I own a furniture manufacturing company in Warsaw, at least I'm half-owner with my partner. She takes care of the production side and I'm the Sales Director. I'm going to Stockholm to see some potential distributors for the Scandinavian market.

IJ   What sort of furniture does your company make?

EK   Mainly office furniture. We try to be as innovative as possible. Get away from the usual brown and black colours. In materials too, we're using some very interesting new plastics that don't look like plastic. *[Really?]* I've got a catalogue here if you're interested.

IJ   Mmm … it looks very interesting. What sort of turnover do you have?

EK   You mean sales? The equivalent of about 30 million euros a year.

IJ   How long have you been in business?

EK   We started out in 1993. We've been dealing mainly with the European market so far, and we're looking to expand elsewhere, obviously.

IJ   Mmm … Very interesting. Well, as you probably know, we have 50 stores worldwide. We're trying to develop the ranges of office furniture we sell. I think our chief buyer in Stockholm would be very interested to meet you: Agneta Dahlquist. You must come over and see her. How about this week?

EK   Tomorrow is going to be difficult. How about the day after, in the afternoon?

IJ   Why don't you come out to our offices in Solna at, say, two o'clock on Thursday, then? They're right next to Solna underground station. Solna's about 30 minutes from central Stockholm.

EK   I'll look forward to that. Here's my card.

IJ   Ah, Meblopol. I've seen that name somewhere. And here's mine.

EK   Thanks.

IJ   Looks as though we'll be arriving early. That's unusual these days …

Exercise 4

IJ = Ingvar Jonsson
EW = Ewa Kowalska
AD = Agneta Dahlquist

IJ   Hello, Ewa. You found us OK then.

EK   Yes, no problem at all.

IJ   Let me introduce you to Agneta Dahlquist. She's our chief furniture buyer.

EK   Hello.

AD   Nice to meet you.

IJ   And now, if you'll excuse me, I'll leave you two to it.

EK   Thanks. And thanks again for asking me out here.

IJ   My pleasure. I hope we can do business together. Bye for now.

EK   Bye.

AD   Let's go up to my office.

EK   Fine.

AD   Can I get you something? Tea, coffee, juice, mineral water?

EK   Some juice would be good.

AD   Here you go.

EK   Thanks.

AD   Ingvar told me that you met on the plane from Warsaw. Is this your first time in Stockholm?

EK   No, I've been here a couple of times recently on business trips, but they didn't lead to anything, unfortunately.

AD   Well, maybe this time. Shall we get down to business?

Answer key

UNIT 1

A Listening

2
B 3, 5, 6
C 1, 3, 7
D 3, 5, 8, 9, 10

3
1, 2, 3, 5, 6, 9, 10

4
1 c   2 b   3 b   4 a   5 c   6 b
7 c   8 b   9 c   10 a

5
1 T   2 F   3 T   4 T   5 F   6 F

B Reading and writing

KEY VOCABULARY
a) beautiful, good-looking
b) innovative, revolutionary
c) economical, efficient
d) robust
e) reliable
f) compact
g) powerful

1
1 b   2 d   3 b   4 c   5 b   6 a
7 d   8 b   9 a   10 b   11 d

2
2 it   5 off
3 of   6 on
4 a

C Speaking

1
Possible answers

Delivery of goods
when the goods are delivered, they are
    damaged
when the goods are delivered, some items
    are missing

Product performance: computers
the computer keeps on crashing (suddenly
    ceasing to work)
you try to do a particular task, like printing
    something, but nothing happens

Service performance: car mechanics
they replace parts that don't need replacing
they charge too much for the work they do

Service performance: banks
you ask the bank to transfer money from
    one account to a second account, but
    instead they transfer it from the second
    account to the first account
you want to transfer a small amount of
    money abroad, but the charge for sending
    it is almost as much as the amount to be
    sent

Product and service performance: clothes
you buy something and the first time you
    wash it, it shrinks
you buy a shirt, wear it once and the
    buttons start falling off

UNIT 2

A Reading and writing

KEY VOCABULARY
1 a   2 c   3 b   4 a   5 b   6 c

1
1 b   2 e   3 c   4 a

2
1 c   2 f   3 a   4 g

3
Model answer
Marmaris is a resort in south-west Turkey.
You can fly there directly from many
European cities. The summers are very hot,
and the winters are mild with some rain.
The main tourist season is from March to
November. There are a lot of good hotels on
the coast near the town. There are some
good restaurants and night clubs in the
town itself. Sports include windsurfing,
water-skiing and diving. The resort has
grown very fast in recent years. In 1980,
there were 10 yachts in the harbour each
evening in summer. Now there are 300.

B Listening

1
A 5   B 4   C 3   D 6   E 7   F 8

2
1 T   2 T   3 DK   4 F   5 DK
6 F   7 F   8 DK   9 T   10 T

3
 2 I'll put you through.
 3 Hi, Stavros, it's Al Palmer. How are
    you?
 4 How's the weather over there?
 5 Of course, there are some points we
    must talk about in more detail.
 6 That's inevitable. But you like the overall
    idea?
 7 How about coming over here to discuss
    things in the next couple of weeks?
 8 It'll be great to see you over here.
 9 We'll arrange for someone to meet you.
10 OK, my personal assistant will be in
    touch soon with our arrangements.

4
Name of hotel: Khania Palace
Names of guests: Alvin Palmer and
    Jerry Salinas
Date of arrival: December 4th
Date of departure: December 7th
Room rate: 110 euros
Breakfast included? yes
Special requests: a quiet room for
    Mr Palmer
Hotel's e-mail address:
reception@khaniapalace.gr

C Speaking

KEY VOCABULARY
1 arrivals hall – b
2 check-in desk – d
3 connecting flight – f
4 departure lounge – e
5 flight number – c
6 transfer passengers – a

UNIT 3

A Listening

KEY VOCABULARY
The economy
1 E   2 G   3 F   4 A   5 H   6 D
7 B   8 C

Industries
1 F   2 D   3 E   4 G   5 C   6 A
7 B

1
 1 Spanish   9 Hindi
 2 17th   10 5–6%
 3 40%   11 4%
 4 30%   12 3%
 5 20%   13 22
 6 6%   14 electronics
 7 Spanish   15 tourism
 8 Chinese

2
go up / went up / gone up / —
rise / rose / risen / rise
increase / increased / increased /
    increase
grow / grew / grown / growth
go down / went down / gone down /
    —
fall / fell / fallen / fall
decrease / decreased / decreased /
    decrease
drop / dropped / dropped / drop
reach / reached / reached / —

3

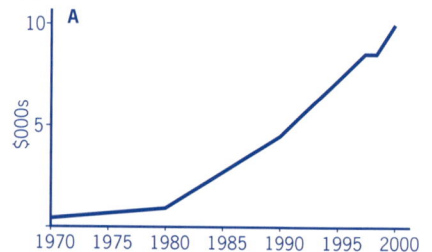

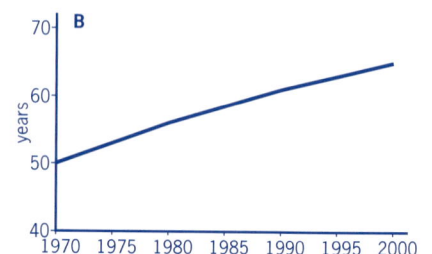

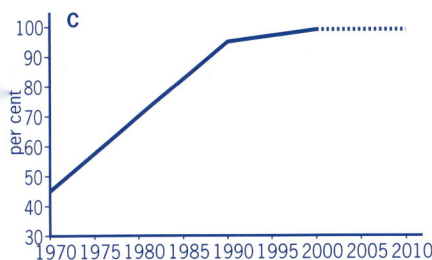

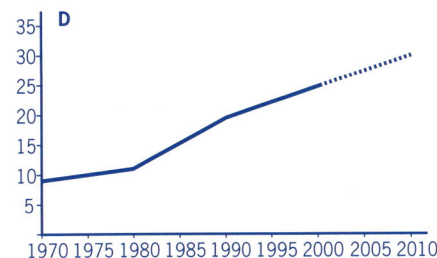

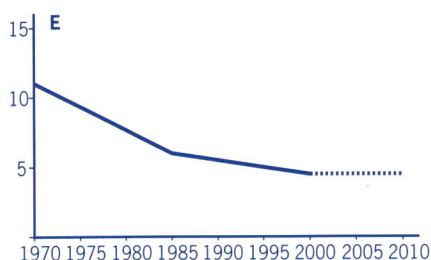

C

(graph with y-axis "per cent" from 30 to 100, x-axis 1970–2010)

D

(graph with y-axis 5 to 35, x-axis 1970–2010)

E

(graph with y-axis 5 to 15, x-axis 1970–2010)

B Speaking

KEY VOCABULARY
Graphs and charts
1 bar chart
2 pie chart
3 vertical axis
4 horizontal axis
5 line graph

Comparisons and trends
1 a   2 b   3 c   4 b   5 c   6 b
7 b

C Reading and writing

KEY VOCABULARY
1 living standards
2 prosperity
3 environment
4 quality of life
5 stress
6 poverty
7 development
8 prosperous

1
1 T   2 F   3 F   4 DK   5 F   6 T
7 T   8 DK   9 T   10 F   11 T
12 DK

2
a 4   b 1   c ✗   d ✗   e 3   f 2

3
2 the   5 for
3 is   6 to
4 do

4
Model answer
Fishing and tourism will be badly affected if the project is allowed to go ahead.

We should protest as strongly as possible against the project, for example by writing to the Ministry of the Environment, organising

---

a petition, and by demonstrating in the street so that the authorities know how strongly we feel about the issue.

More and more people feel strongly about protecting the environment. If we organise our protests well, we will be able to stop the refinery from being built.

UNIT 4

A Reading and writing

KEY VOCABULARY
1 inward investment – d
2 job creation – e
3 recruitment drive – a
4 skilled workforce – c
5 hi-tech industry – b

1
1 c   2 a   3 b   4 d   5 b   6 a
7 d   8 c   9 c   10 a

2
2 longing: long
3 high: highly
4 experiments: experience
5 automation: automated
6 equipments: equipment
7 jobs: job
8 hugely: huge
9 govern's: government's
10 projection: project

3
Model answer
Dear Sir or Madam,

I recently saw in a newspaper article that you are opening a plant in the Dublin area, and I would like to apply for a job as a staff trainer at Random. I'm available to start immediately. I have a background in technical training in various computer companies in Ireland and the UK, and I think this would be relevant in training staff at your company. Please find enclosed my CV.

Yours faithfully,

B Reading and speaking

KEY VOCABULARY
1 C   2 D   3 E   4 A   5 G   6 F
7 B

1
A safety standards, equipment maintenance
B continuous supply, raw materials, materials inventory, key suppliers
C –
D advanced manufacturing

2
1 A, D   2 B, D   3 A   4 C   5 B

C Listening

KEY VOCABULARY
2 CANTEEN
3 RECEPTION
4 RESEARCH AND DEVELOPMENT LABORATORY
5 MANUFACTURING PLANT
6 TRAINING CENTRE
7 GYM

1
1 D   2 E   3 B   4 F   5 C
6 A

2
7 canteen
3 company gym
6 packing area
5 production area
1 reception area
2 research and development laboratories
4 training centre

3
1 a   2 c   3 c   4 b   5 a   6 a
7 a   8 b   9 b   10 b

UNIT 5

KEY VOCABULARY
1 B   2 D   3 G   4 F   5 A   6 E
7 C

A Listening

1
4 businesswoman
5 student
2 retired woman
3 executive from a large company
1 self-employed business consultant
6 unemployed man

2
Unemployed man / Malaga / holiday / NG / 7
Businesswoman / Stockholm / NG / NG / 10
Executive / Frankfurt / visiting new colleagues / £70 / NG
Student / Milan / flying back to Milan after seeing parents / £37 / 8
Business consultant / Aberdeen / consultancy work / £35 / 9
Retired woman / Madrid / visiting daughter / £52 / 8

3
cartel, competition, deregulation, monopoly, market leaders

4
1 c   2 c   3 b   4 a   5 c   6 b
7 c   8 a   9 b   10 a

B Speaking

KEY VOCABULARY
1 entrepreneur
2 hi-tech
3 venture capitalists
4 start-ups
5 growth

KEY QUESTIONS AND ANSWERS
1 What's Arturo's background? – e
2 When did Belinda start her company? – c
3 Where did Carlos get the finance to start his company? – g
4 What had Dagmar done before starting her company? – a
5 What does the company do/make? – f
6 Where is the company based? – d
7 What is the value of the company now? – b

C Reading and writing

1

1 h 2 g 3 d 4 f 5 c 6 a

2

1 e 2 c 3 b

3

1 as 4 for
2 for 5 in
3 ✓

4

Model answer

Dear Ms Lambert,

Thank you for your e-mail. Unfortunately I won't be able to come to give a presentation on 15 January as I am seeing a potentially important customer that day, the buyer for a big supermarket chain.

Any other day during the week beginning 15 January would be possible.

I apologise for any inconvenience this may cause.

Best wishes,

UNIT 6

A Listening

KEY VOCABULARY

1 self-employed person – b
2 office furniture – c
3 laptop computer – a
4 home working – d
5 computer network – e
6 coffee machine – f

1

2 head of large company
5 self-employed person
6 advertising executive
3 office manager
4 secretary
1 salesperson

2

1 b 2 b 3 c 4 b 5 a 6 a
7 b 8 a 9 c 10 b

B Speaking

KEY VOCABULARY

Scenario 1: g, f, e, b, d
Scenario 2: g, f, e, b, c, a

KEY QUESTIONS AND ANSWERS

1 B 2 C 3 A 4 E 5 F
6 H 7 D 8 G

C Reading and writing

2

a ✗ b 2 c 3 d ✗ e 4 f ✗
g 1

3

1 c 2 g 3 d 4 e 5 a 6 f

4

Model answer

Dear Mr Roselli,

I saw your company featured in a trade magazine and wondered if you would be interested in our products. I am the co-founder of a company based in Warsaw

called Meblopol. We make and supply furniture for the international market.

We are hoping to expand further and would like to start selling our products in southern Europe, especially Italy. I will be in Italy next week. Would it be possible to meet in Milan on Thursday or Friday?

I'm enclosing a copy of our current catalogue so that you can get an idea of our products.

Looking forward to hearing from you,

Yours sincerely,

Ewa Kowalska

UNIT 7

A Reading and writing

KEY VOCABULARY

1 grew 5 boom
2 grown 6 levels off
3 growth 7 boom and bust
4 takes off

1

1 F 2 F 3 T 4 T 5 F 6 T
7 F 8 F 9 F 10 T

2

1 f 2 d 3 c 4 b

3

Model answer

Dear Ms Harris,

I'm interested in the possibility of becoming a franchisee of your system. I'd like to open a franchise in Darwin. I have had my own business for the last three years, with two employees. Before that I had ten years' experience of installing kitchens for another company. I have A$50,000 of capital available. Is this sufficient to open a franchise?

I'd be grateful if you could phone me on Darwin (08) 3452 8934 to discuss possibilities.

Best wishes,

B Speaking

KEY VOCABULARY

1 B 2 A 3 F 4 C 5 D 6 E

C Listening

1

1 e 2 a 3 ✗ 4 d 5 b

2

a 5 b 3 c 2 d 1 e 4

3

a, b, d, f, h, i, l

4

1 c 2 b 3 b 4 b 5 a 6 c
7 a 8 a 9 b 10 c

UNIT 8

A Listening

KEY EXPRESSIONS

1 E 2 D 3 F 4 G 5 C
6 A 7 B

1

3, 4, 6

KEY VOCABULARY

1 phases/stages
2 stages/phases
3 parallel
4 schedule
5 completion
6 ahead of schedule
7 behind schedule/delayed
8 delayed/behind schedule
9 lead-time

2

1 building engineer
2 airline pilot
3 teacher
4 computer programmer
5 author

3

c 3 d 6 e 4 f 7 g 5 h 8

B Reading and writing

KEY VOCABULARY

1 spending 5 overspend
2 income 6 over budget
3 underspend 7 overrun
4 under budget

1

1 a 2 a 3 b 4 a 5 d 6 d
7 b 8 b 9 a 10 d 11 c
12 d

2

1 F 2 F 3 T 4 F 5 F 6 T
7 F 8 T 9 T 10 T

3

Model answer

Dear Sir or Madam,

I work for a tour operator here in Germany. I have heard from a friend who visited Crete recently that there is a new golf course near Khania. Is there a brochure about this course, and if so, please can you send us 5,000 copies? Does the course offer special rates to tour operators who send visitors there? Please could you also send 5,000 brochures about Khania in general. Could you let me know which hotels are the best for golfers using the course to stay at?

Many thanks,

Best wishes,

4

Model answer

Dear _____,

Many thanks for your inquiry about the possibilities for golf in Khania. The course you mention is now fully open and operating very successfully. I will send you 5,000 copies of the golf course brochure today. With regard to your question about discounts, please contact the golf course directly. Our brochure about Khania in general is currently being reprinted: I will send you 5,000 copies next month as soon as it becomes available. You will find information about suitable hotels for your clients wishing to play golf on the attached list, the next page of this fax.

If you require any further information, please don't hestitate to get in touch.

Best wishes,

C Speaking

KEY VOCABULARY
1 air-conditioning – c
2 full board – f
3 reception desk – e
4 room service – a
5 sports facilities – d
6 swimming pool – b

UNIT 9

A Listening

KEY VOCABULARY
1 opponents, opposition
2 extremists, extreme
3 protesters, protests
4 demonstrators, demonstrate
5 confrontation
6 clash
7 riots, rioters
8 looters

1
1 g   2 a   3 b   4 h   5 d

2
1 a   2 a   3 c   4 b   5 c   6 b

3
1 T   2 T   3 T   4 F   5 F   6 T
7 T   8 F   9 T   10 DK

B Speaking

KEY EXPRESSIONS
Making your point
1 H   2 A   3 D   4 B   5 C   6 G
7 E   8 F

Developing your point
1 B   2 C   3 A   4 G   5 F   6 D
7 H   8 E

C Reading and writing

KEY VOCABULARY
1 consulted
2 modified
3 carried out
4 imposed
5 dropped
6 rejected, thrown out

1
1 g   2 b   3 d   4 f   5 e

2
1 c   2 d   3 g   4 e

3
Model answer
To: Mary Goncalves, Green Action
I own and run a hotel on the west coast of Hermosa. I support the government's proposals for the new motorway and for expanding the airport for the following reasons.

1. The new motorway is required because the existing road is very dangerous. Tourists spend a lot of time stuck in traffic jams. The new motorway will bring new jobs to the west coast in the short term and allow the area to be opened up for tourism in the longer term.

2. The airport expansion is needed because the existing airport is very crowded and congested, with a lot of delays. People get a very negative first impression of Hermosa when they arrive. What's more, bigger jets cannot use the existing airport, and this will slow down the development of tourism in the area.

I hope that Green Action will consider these points, and change its position on the development of the west coast.

UNIT 10

A Listening

KEY VOCABULARY
1 demand   4 recession
2 boom   5 slump
3 demand   6 downturns

1
2 cinemas –
3 pig farming –
4 clothes +
5 personal computers –

KEY VOCABULARY
1 b   2 b   3 a   4 b   5 c   6 c
7 c

2
1 F   2 F   3 T   4 F   5 F   6 T
7 T   8 F   9 T   10 T

B Reading and writing

KEY VOCABULARY
1 relocation costs – c
2 redundancy package – b
3 payroll cuts – e
4 outplacement services – d
5 salary costs – f
6 human resources – a

1
1 b   2 a   3 c   4 d   5 d
6 b   7 c   8 a   9 b   10 a

2
1 F   2 F   3 T   4 T   5 F
6 T   7 T   8 F   9 T   10 F

3
Model answer
Dear Ms O'Reilly,

Thank you for your letter of June 6. I'm writing to let you know that I think Random is making a big mistake in making experienced employees redundant. The voluntary redundancy package is nothing more than a form of bribe. I'm sure that the current problems experienced by Random are only temporary, and that the company should keep as many employees as possible, so as to be ready for an improvement in business.

Personally, I do not wish to accept the redundancy package.

Yours sincerely,

4
Model answer
Dear Ms O'Reilly,

Thank you for your letter of June 6, offering a voluntary redundancy package. I would like to accept this offer. Would it be possible to arrange an appointment with someone in the human resources department in order to discuss the package?

Meanwhile, please could you let me know what sort of services the outplacement consultancy mentioned in your letter can offer? In addition, I'd like to know how much you are willing to pay for relocation costs.

Like you, I feel disappointed that these redundancies have become necessary.

Looking forward to hearing from you,

Yours sincerely,

C Speaking

KEY VOCABULARY
1 motivation   4 incentive
2 committed   5 morale
3 perform

KEY QUESTIONS AND ANSWERS
1 E   2 A   3 B   4 C   5 D

UNIT 11

A Listening

KEY VOCABULARY
1 target company   5 predator
2 takeover   6 prey
3 friendly   7 merger
4 acquisitions

1
1 Pierre Martin / Geneva Business Daily / 00 41 22 769 4341 / arrange an interview
2 Suzanne Byers / Clifton Lansdown / 01865 508318 / clarify details in legal documents
3 Brian Jack / Financial Press / 020 7908 3529 / arrange an interview
4 Joe / NG / NG / arrange a game of tennis
5 Marie-Claire Allain / White Cross Airways / NG / arrange lunch at the Savoy to discuss strategy

2
1 100 million Swiss francs
2 7 million Swiss francs
3 10
4 several million
5 3 or 4
6 7 million
7 over 60 million
8 160,000
9 450,000

3
1 b   2 c   3 b   4 b   5 c   6 b
7 b   8 a   9 c   10 b

B Reading and writing

1
1 Croydon airport (F); Central London (AA)
2 Croydon airport (F); Gatwick airport (AA)
3 7 years (F); nearly 20 years (AA)
4 less than other airlines (F); average (AA)
5 33 (F); NM (AA)
6 by phone and over the internet (F); through travel agents, sales offices and, recently, over the internet (AA)

7 no, only coffee (F); yes (AA)
8 good (F); NM (AA)

2
1 c   2 a   3 h   4 b   5 g

3
Model answer
You know the company I was working for merged with another company six months ago. Well, the companies had two very different styles. The people from the other company dressed too casually: the men didn't wear ties and the women wore jeans to the office. I didn't like the way they talked to each other: they were too familiar and didn't show enough respect to others, especially the people above them. They always turned up five or ten minutes late for meetings. And in the meetings, they were always interrupting, not allowing others to finish what they had to say. I got the impression they didn't work hard enough: they went home much earlier than we used to in our company before the merger.

Anyway, I've had enough, and I'm looking for another job. I want to work for a company with more traditional values.

All the best,

C Speaking

KEY VOCABULARY
1 action
2 carried out
3 effective
4 planned
5 consequences
6 foreseen
7 intended

UNIT 12

A Listening

KEY EXPRESSIONS
1 B   2 C   3 A   4 G   5 D   6 E
7 F

1
Financial Press
Ingvar Jonsson
Ewa Kowalska
Agneta Dahlquist
Solna
Meblopol

2
1 T   2 F   3 T   4 F   5 T   6 F
7 F   8 T   9 T   10 F   11 T
12 F

3
1 b   2 c   3 b   4 a   5 c   6 b

4
1 ✓
2 Let me introduce you to Agneta Dahlquist.
3 And now, if you'll excuse me, I'll leave you two to it.
4 Thanks again for asking me out here.
5 ✓
6 Let's go up to my office.
7 ✓
8 Shall we get down to business?

B Speaking and writing

KEY EXPRESSIONS
1 B   2 G   3 A   4 C   5 D   6 E
7 F

a) 6 E   e) 5 D
b) 2 G   f) 7 F
c) 3 A   g) 1 B
d) 4 C

3
Model answer
It was very nice meeting you the other day. This is to summarise briefly what we decided about the supply of desks by your company.

We agreed on a wholesale price of 205 euros per unit, with your company supplying 17,500 units per year.

The duration of this agreement is to be three years. Delivery is to begin in three months.

Looking forward to working with you,

Best wishes,

C Reading and writing

KEY VOCABULARY
1 B   2 A   3 D   4 C   5 F   6 E

1
1 to   4 ✓
2 with   5 to
3 of   6 for

2
1 d   2 b   3 a   4 b   5 d   6 a
7 d

DELTA Publishing
39 Alexandra Road
Addlestone
Surrey KT15 2PQ
United Kingdom

Text © Bill Mascull 2000

Design and illustration © Delta Publishing 2000

German edition published by Max Hueber Verlag, D–85737 Ismaning

First published 2000
International edition ISBN 1 900783 43 6
German edition ISBN 3-19-002704-X

Design and illustration by Oxford Designers & Illustrators
Printed in Malta by Interprint Limited

Photograph acknowledgements
The author and publishers wish to acknowledge, with thanks, the following photographic sources:

Art Directors and TRIP Photograph Library pp 6 right (photograph G Grieves); 8 (photograph R Ewing); 12 (photograph H Rogers); 20 (photograph R Nichols); 27 (photograph S Grant); 29 (photograph H Rogers); 37 left & centre (photographs H Rogers); 37 right (photograph T Sims); 38 (photograph R Brown); 48 (photograph H Rogers); 66 (photograph International Color Stock); 72 (photograph C Ryan)

DESIGNS FOR LIVING, Wokingham pp 4; 6 left; 42 (photographs Studio Carr Ltd)

FORMAT Photographers Ltd p 61 (photograph Raisa Page)

Clive Frost p 34

Christine Osborne Pictures p 46

Popperfoto pp 52 (photograph Reuters/Andy Clark); 58

Xilinx Ireland Offices in Citywest Business Campus in Dublin p 23 (photograph Frank Fennell)

The publishers have made every effort to trace the copyright holders, but if they have inadvertently overlooked any, they will be pleased to make the necessary arrangements at the first opportunity.